THE COVERED BRIDGES OF ASHTABULA COUNTY, OHIO

CARL E. FEATHER

Published by The History Press
Charleston, SC 29403
www.historypress.net

Copyright © 2014 by Carl E. Feather
All rights reserved

Cover images by Carl E. Feather.

First published 2014

Manufactured in the United States

ISBN 978.1.62619.261.4

Library of Congress CIP data applied for.

Notice: The information in this book is true and complete to the best of our knowledge. It is offered without guarantee on the part of the author or The History Press. The author and The History Press disclaim all liability in connection with the use of this book.

All rights reserved. No part of this book may be reproduced or transmitted in any form whatsoever without prior written permission from the publisher except in the case of brief quotations embodied in critical articles and reviews.

To my father, Carl J. Feather, my bridge to the past;

To my son, Aaron E. Feather, and my grandson, Mason L. Feather, my bridges to the future.

CONTENTS

Acknowledgements	7
Introduction	9
The Need for Bridges	11
Trusses and Builders	21
Forgotten Crossings: The Lost Bridges	37
The Honored Dozen: Saving What Remained	81
New Construction: John Smolen Jr. and Timber Bridge Revival	107
Longest, Shortest	115
Merely a Mention	125
Notes	131
Bibliography	133
Index	137
About the Author	143

ACKNOWLEDGEMENTS

Ashtabula County historian Alice Bliss did a superb job of researching all of the county's covered bridges and serializing her work in Ashtabula County newspapers in the late 1960s. Walter Jack, a newspaperman and photographer, documented in words and images the covered bridges of both Ashtabula (Ohio) and Erie (Pennsylvania) Counties, even as they were disappearing from the scene in the 1930s and 1940s. More recently, Dennis Osborn painstakingly researched both the byway and railroad covered bridges that have received *World Guide to Covered Bridges* numbers. Their research provided the starting point for my work of tracking down more details and stories while updating the state of covered bridges in Ashtabula County during the past fifty years.

Norma Waters of the Jefferson Historical Society has spent thousands of hours harvesting tidbits from the pages of nineteenth-century Ashtabula County newspapers. On many occasions, as I attempted to complete the half-worked puzzles left behind by other writers, one of Norma's purple cards mentioning a bridge or an event provided a missing piece.

The Olin Museum of Covered Bridges provided several photographs for this book, as did Dean Luce of North Kingsville, whose late father, Edward M. "Ned" Luce, was county road supervisor and engineer. The records of the Ashtabula County Covered Bridge Festival are on file in the Jefferson Historical Society's research library, and they provided photographs of several "forgotten crossings." The Ashtabula County Engineer's Office also opened its files of documentation, newspaper clippings and images for this work.

Acknowledgements

Karen Rang, the granddaughter of Walter Jack, graciously allowed contact prints to be made from his original camera negatives from 1930 to 1950, thereby providing readers with a fresh look at old bridges.

Todd Clark of Cincinnati, a collector of covered bridge photographs, kindly supplied images of several extinct bridges from more than a century ago. Todd's collection is amazing, exceeded only by his willingness to share his trove with other historians.

The Internet is a wonderful research tool, and I am especially grateful for www.lostbridges.org, which is the work of New Hampshire resident Bill Caswell. Also, a tip of the hat goes to Dale J. Travis (dalejtravis.com) and his online lists of covered bridges and round barns, as well as the Ohio Historic Bridge Association (oldohiobridges.com).

Greg Dumais, my commissioning editor, and the rest of The History Press staff have been a pleasure to work with. I thank them for helping me bring this long-latent work to light.

Finally, an author is always indebted to the patience of his family whenever a work is in progress. To my parents, son and grandson, I say thank you for giving me the space and understanding that allowed me to complete this work. And to my wife, Amanda, I give special gratitude for her patience and willingness to give me the space to work and her professional editing skills, as well as giving me the confidence to tackle the project. Thank you for being my best friend and copy editor.

INTRODUCTION

Snow has been falling on the rural township all afternoon, yet my subcompact car's tires create the first set of tracks in it. The temperature is fifteen degrees, and the parting clouds suggest even colder temperatures are descending like the snow. I pull off the road—onto what I trust is a berm and not a ditch—and prepare to work.

The glow of a flat-screen television pours from the living room windows of a McMansion high above the creek bed. The yelps of a dog, perhaps a coyote, echo down the valley. The light is fading quickly. By the time I position my tripod, double-check the focus on my lens and verify the wireless connections, the environment will have changed dramatically. In that darkness peculiar to the rural landscape, the only reality to my camera will be what I illuminate with my strobes.

Why have I chosen this night, this cold, this snow in which to document something that has been here for more than a century and, fire and flood aside, will remain come June? The answer is in my obsession with these structures—wooden time tunnels, as I am inclined to call them. They have been my neighbors since my parents moved to this county more than fifty-five years ago, although some have faded from the landscape in that time. Taking that lesson from the past, I photograph those that remain, knowing that nothing lasts forever.

Having grown tired of producing "sunny 16" images, I turned in 2011 to photographing the county's covered bridges at night, using the selective nighttime lighting techniques mastered by O. Winston Link. Since starting

INTRODUCTION

this project, I have become much more intimate with the details of Ashtabula County's covered bridges. Nighttime photography forces me to study each bridge ahead of time and decide what features will be illuminated, and thus emphasized, and which will receive only a nod or total disregard. As a result, I have gained an even greater respect for the workmanship of these structures and the men who built them using only basic tools and rivulets of sweat.

Time thus spent in the presence of these functional monuments convinced me that each one possesses a personality and a story. And that is what this book is about—not a mere rehashing of construction dates and measurements but rather portraits of these structures and a tribute to their mostly anonymous builders. The county's twelve historical covered bridges are particularly worthy of this honor. They are the only surviving offspring of a romance between a heavily timbered landscape and a race determined to subdue it. We are the blessed heirs of that union, benefactors to a rich heritage bequeathed by displaced New Englanders whose communities are but long shadows cast by their hometowns to the east by hope's sunrise: Windsor, Andover, New Lyme, Colebrook and Dorset. Town squares, town halls, Congregational churches and covered bridges—their legacy lives on in name and wood.

At least forty-eight wood-truss bridges once stood on the highways of Ashtabula County. Only twelve remain. The future will never give us more of the past than what we hold today, and we must live each day with that reality. Yes, we can and have constructed new timber bridges, and this volume tells their stories as well. But their timbers sprouted and grew in soil far from the rivers they cross, and their trusses were birthed with cranes rather than groans and grind. The historical bridges are treasures that no amount of money can buy, for while we cannot purchase the past, we can honor what is left of it.

To step into the world of the covered bridge is, therefore, to step into the strong arms of history. And it is there where we begin our journey.

THE NEED FOR BRIDGES

Covered bridges are one of the few links with the past still existing today. While their role as a carrier of traffic is certainly doomed, their place as a link with the pioneering spirit of America should not be wiped from the face of the earth. The steam locomotive, once an everyday sight, has become a museum piece. Under the invincible juggernaut of progress, the covered bridge is about to follow it.
—Bill Reynard, Star-Beacon, *"Efforts Being Made to Preserve Bridges,"*
October 12, 1963

Newspaperman Bill Reynard got it right on two out of three counts: covered bridges are links to the past, and for that reason alone, they ought not to be "wiped from the face of the earth."

Despite Reynard's fear of the invincible juggernaut of progress in the Buckeye State, the covered bridge is far from extinct in Ohio. According to the Ohio Historic Bridge Association, there were 127 publicly accessible timber truss bridges standing in Ohio as of the summer of 2013. Another 18 or so stood on private property.

Ironically, nowhere else in the nation did Bill Reynard's prophecy about "doomed" wooden bridges fall more short of truth than in the very Ohio county where his words were published. Twelve of the sixteen covered bridges that stood in Ashtabula County when he wrote his stories still stand, eleven of them providing passage over the county's streams and rivers. The retired bridge is the centerpiece of a metro park. And since 1984, six new timber bridges, including the longest and shortest in the nation, have been built.

THE COVERED BRIDGES OF ASHTABULA COUNTY, OHIO

The Wiswell Road covered bridge in southern Ashtabula County dates back to 1867, but thanks to regular maintenance and restoration work, it continues to provide safe passage over Phelps Creek for both man and beast. *Photo by author.*

The eighteen bridges in this northeast Ohio county have earned it the nickname "Covered Bridge Capital of Ohio," with a caveat. Fairfield County, also in Ohio, has eighteen covered bridges as well. However, some of Fairfield's bridges are restricted to pedestrian traffic, and some are completely out of service or on private property.

While the suggestion of a modern bridge still being in service 150 years from now seems as unlikely as steam locomotives making a revival, it would not surprise their builders. They revered wood and respected its potential when used in structures properly engineered and shielded from the elements. Without taking both factors into consideration, wood, by its very nature, must go the way of flesh rather than bone.

This, then, is the primary reason these timber bridges have a roof, a covering. It is there to protect the load-bearing elements—the beams or chords that stretch across the span, the trusses that distribute the tension and compression and the floor that receives the burden. No matter how hardy the species used for these elements, wood is subject to weather-induced decay, especially at points of joinery. And so it is that the covered bridge,

The Need for Bridges

often made from several species of wood cut and drilled to the needs of the builder, is a body of many parts, the sum of which provides safe crossing.

There are, of course, many rustic if not romantic notions about covering a bridge. Some will claim that the covering and walls made it easier to drive skittish livestock across a raging river or that the bridge provided a convenient shelter from the elements in horse-and-buggy days. More ridiculous is the "wishing bridge" concept—if you make a wish as you cross the old wooden bridge, the wish will come true. Perhaps that stems from the poor condition into which many of the neglected bridges fell in their later days—the motorist's wish was that the bridge would hold the weight of his vehicle.

And there are the tales of "kissing bridges," so named because they provided the venue for a bashful couple to steal a kiss amid the dark shadows. Perhaps there is some truth to this, for one need only walk the length of an old bridge's interior to see the love stories contained amid the grain and dust—"L.C. loves A.D forever," "E.M. + D.J." and more. There are stories in these timbers, make no mistake about that. Yet no matter how much one cares to idealize the covered bridge, the fact of the matter is that their builders and users could not afford nonfunctional embellishments. In most cases, public money was being spent on these bridges, and taxpayers, especially those of Yankee stock, are quick to spot a wasted nickel. Many of Ashtabula County's legacy bridges went for want of paint most of their lives.

Practicality also dictated the width of these bridges. Any width greater than that sufficient for a hay wagon loaded to the hilt was a waste—thus, with the notable exception of two "double barrel" covered bridges that once stood in the county, the legacy bridges present a tight squeeze. Further, many of these structures require a sharp turn to access, creating a tight curve and blind spot for the driver entering the bridge. You can always spot a motorist who learned to drive in covered-bridge country: he turns on the vehicle's headlamps and toots the horn before entering the crossing.

There were bridge customs and courtesies in the olden days as well. Signs posted on the portal warned of a "$5 fine for riding or driving on this bridge faster than a walk," as if a horse-riding constable with a radar gun was waiting on the other side. The reason for this warning was to prevent damage to the bridge from the rapid pounding of horse hooves that otherwise would cause the bridge to shake and thereby damage joints. Even soldiers were told to "break step" when crossing the bridges in file.

Despite our tendency to refer to the "slower paced days of the past," our rural-dwelling ancestors, forever feeling the pressure of unpredictable weather, were not ones to waste time. At harvest time, the covered bridge, with its narrow portal, was a bottleneck. The courtesy of the byway was "first come, first cross," and the approaching team or rider had the responsibility for making sure that the way was clear. Failure to do so could result in a verbal exchange or worse between the impatient farmers.

Another source of concern was the horse or team that became "spooked" as it approached or exited the bridge. The *Ashtabula News* of May 2, 1878, tells this story of a crossing that went poorly due to a horse's misstep:

> *On Saturday last, as Mr. Bird Chapin with his wife and babe were going to Dorset Center, and just as they had passed out of the covered bridge near the old Collins farm, the horse gave a sudden jump and plunged off the south side of the embankment, throwing Mr. Chapin out into the creek and jerking the reins out of his hands. The horse stumbled a little, but rallied and turned, ran up the ditch a little and out into the road again, and ran clear to the store, where he was caught by Mr. John Burr. Fortunately, the buggy was not upset, and Mrs. C. succeeded in keeping herself and child in the buggy, the lines all the time dragging on the ground. Mr. C. picked himself out of the creek, and followed as fast as he could burdened as he was with wet clothes and boots full of water. They were none of them hurt, but pretty muddy and wet, and nothing about buggy or harness was broken. An hour or two after, Henry Porter, passing the scene of the accident, saw something in the water, and fishing it out it proved to be Mr. C.'s overcoat, which was on the buggy seat when the horse threw him out.*

Wood, Water and Wagons

Bridges are geography's tax on mankind's determination to tame a well-watered wilderness. The three main waterways in Ashtabula County are the Ashtabula River, Conneaut Creek and the Grand River. As its name suggests, the Grand River is the most challenging of the three. Born in Geauga County, to the southwest of Ashtabula County, the Grand meanders through western Ashtabula County before taking a turn to the west a few miles shy of reaching Lake Erie. It completes its journey through Lake County, meeting Lake Erie at Fairport Harbor. It was the first river in Ashtabula County to receive the Ohio Department of Natural Resources' "State Wild and Scenic" river designation, which was bestowed in 1974.

The Need for Bridges

The State Road covered bridge spans Conneaut Creek, a "Wild and Scenic" river. The bridge is a Town lattice structure that was built in 1983. Its construction marked the beginning of a covered bridge revival in Ashtabula County. *Photo by author.*

Conneaut Creek, on the opposite side of the county, is also designated Wild and Scenic. With headwaters in Pennsylvania, the creek presented an obstacle in two states. During the creek's twenty-two-mile journey through Ohio, it has encountered covered bridges at nine crossing points, including a curious twin-bridge crossing at a point known as Farnham.

The Ashtabula River's name is Native American in origin and means "river of many fish." It could just as well mean river of many bridges, for between the main trunk and its two branches, East and West, there have been at least eighteen wooden bridges.

In the county's midsection is Mill Creek, a Grand River tributary that, after a thunderstorm, flows swiftly with water the color of cappuccino but snoozes like a hound after a hunt during the dog days of August. At least nine covered bridges have known and met the challenges of this little stream, which is particularly frisky by the time it wanders past Jefferson, the county seat.

In the early 1800s, so many mills were built along this Mill Creek that the settlers named it "Mills Creek," said Norma Waters of the Jefferson Historical Society. That presented a problem, however, for there already existed a Mill Creek, which was originally known as Giddings Run and was finally changed to Cemetery Creek. The *s* was lopped off Mills Creek, and the singular version was in use by the time an 1874 atlas of the county was published.

A number of lesser streams also required wooden crossings: Phelps Creek in the southwest corner, Pymatuning Creek in the southeast and Trumbull and Rock Creeks in the midsection. Even little Whitman Creek, which empties into Lake Erie between Conneaut and Ashtabula, once required the services of a covered bridge.

New England Influences

Ashtabula County lies entirely within the Connecticut Western Reserve, a tract of roughly 3 million acres claimed by Connecticut from 1662 to 1800 and lying between the forty-first and forty-second two-minute parallels west of Pennsylvania. King Charles II originally granted the land to Connecticut, which "reserved" a 120-mile-long strip of land along Lake Erie from its western lands ceded to Congress as payment for state war debt. Thus, for several years this "Reserve" operated as a colony of Connecticut until, in 1800, the state relinquished its legal jurisdiction to Congress.

The land became of interest to investors after 1794, the year General Anthony Wayne defeated the confederacy of Native Americans at Fallen Timbers. The treaty that followed in 1795 virtually removed the threat of Indian attack from the Western Reserve and thus "stimulated Connecticut further to formulate a workable method of sale and colonization of her Ohio territory," wrote Harlan Hatcher in *The Western Reserve: The Story of New Connecticut in Ohio*.

The Connecticut Land Company, a group of thirty-five investors, negotiated the price of $1.2 million. On July 4, 1796, a survey party led by General Moses Cleaveland reached the western border of the Reserve and celebrated the beginning of its work, and the nation's twentieth Independence Day, with a round of drinks at Conneaut Creek. The party began its work the next day and named its landing point "Salem," reserving the name "Cleveland" for a city that would be founded on the Cuyahoga River rather than on Conneaut Creek.

These men were not settlers; rather, they were hired to perform the difficult task of surveying this wilderness and marking it off into ranges and townships. The work continued throughout the summer and fall of 1796; a larger group returned the following year and managed to complete the survey of all Reserve lands east of the Cuyahoga River.

Settlement of these lands was not nearly as methodical. Parcels were sold haphazardly across the Reserve, requiring each settler to hack his own way into the wilderness once he left the lakeshore or one of the Indian trails that crisscrossed the region. In March 1797, Alexander Harper of New York, along with twenty-four other adults and children, departed from the "old" Harpersfield in New York for what would become Harpersfield Township in Ashtabula County. Getting to the Reserve was itself a huge task; it took nearly two months to get from Rome, New York, to the Western Reserve.

Asa S. Turney was five years old when he came to the Western Reserve with his parents. Many years after making the trek from Fairfield County, Connecticut, Turney told a biographer for the *History of Geauga and Lake Counties* that "there were then no roads or bridges—simply a wild kind of trail through the woods. The horses and oxen were made to swim the streams, the goods were put aboard such rude boats as could be found in those days, and a line attached to the wagons and drawn across by hand."

Settlement of Ashtabula County, which was formed in 1807 and politically organized on January 22, 1811, moved at a lethargic pace dictated by pathetic road conditions. Nevertheless, the gait increased briskly following the War of 1812, which put to rest the British and Indian issues in the Lake Erie basin. Ashtabula County's population was around 1,000 in 1810; a decade later, it was 7,382, and in 1830, 14,584.

After returning to Connecticut, where he resumed his law practice, Moses Cleaveland worked with the land company to set forth the specifications for a road through the wilderness from the Pennsylvania border to his namesake city, which existed only on paper at that point. In February 1797, the six members of the committee—Seth Pease, Moses Warren, William Shepard Jr., Joseph Perkins, Samuel Hinckley and David Waterman—submitted their report. General Simon Perkins was selected to supervise the effort. Perkins entered the Reserve in 1798, established a camp and began laying out the road according to the plan: "The small stuff [brush] is to be cut out 25-feet wide, and the timber to be girdled 33-feet wide and sufficient bridges thrown over the streams as are not fordable."

This road, which cost $6,000 to build, became known as the Old Girdled Road, the "girdle" referring to the circular cut that was made in the bark and cortex of the trees selected for clearing. It began at the Ohio-Pennsylvania state line (Underridge Road follows this route) and continued west through Kelloggsville, along the present-day Plymouth Ridge, south to Austinburg and through Harpersfield before briefly dipping into Trumbull County and continuing its westward journey toward Cleveland on present-day Euclid Avenue.

The road zigzagged through the county, making the most of natural features that avoided the rivers and hills. Nevertheless, the Old Girdled Road eventually had to ford the Conneaut, Ashtabula and Grand, as well as smaller streams. As was often the case with the early roads in the county, the builders used established Indian trails and fords, the latter eliminating the need for a bridge, except in times of high water. A good ford had to be shallow with a rock bottom for the safety of the horses and livestock; a gentle, sloping approach didn't hurt either.

A second early road went south from Conneaut through Williamsfield Township, in the southeast corner of the county, and on to Kinsman in Trumbull County. Called the Old Salt Road, the trail was built to transport the valuable commodity of salt from Trumbull County. Constructed in 1804, the road followed the eastern portion of the county's higher ridges, virtually eliminating the bridge issue.

One other early road deserves mention as we lay the groundwork for a discussion of covered bridges: the Ashtabula-Trumbull Turnpike. Route 45 follows the course of this old road, which was called the "Woods Road" between Warren, in Trumbull County, to Austinburg, one of the early settlements in Ashtabula County. From Austinburg to Ashtabula, the road was known as yet another "Old Salt Road."

This turnpike was a toll road, authorized by the Ohio legislature in 1818. A stock company received compensation from every user of the road—tollgates were placed at ten-mile intervals. In 1832, those receipts helped build what was probably the first covered bridge in Ashtabula County.

To call any one of these trails a "road" is a disservice to the word, however. Many pioneers, frustrated by the poor road conditions, resorted to traveling along the lakeshore. When Ohio was admitted to the Union in 1803, it had not a single bridge, according to early Ohio historian Caleb Atwater. The task of cutting roads and building bridges fell largely to the nascent local governments and, very often, private subscribers, who pooled financial resources to construct byways and bridges. It was not unusual in those days for a landowner to shoulder the responsibility for cutting a road and building whatever crude bridges were necessary to reach his clearing in the wilderness.

Aaron Wright, Nathan King and Seth Harrington were among the first serious settlers of Salem, which would become Conneaut. In 1800, they

The Need for Bridges

cleared a former Indian trail along the shoreline of an ancient lake. The "South Ridge" thus became the first road to connect the settlements of Conneaut, Ashtabula and Harpersfield. The ridge road, however, skirted the issue of crossing Conneaut Creek by starting west of the creek.

Indeed, ferrying was, in the county's early years, the most efficient, though costly, way to get across the creek. Commissioners in 1815 approved the following rates of ferrying at or near the mouth of "Coneaught Creek" (amounts are in cents):

- a loaded cart or wagon with four horses or oxen   62½
- a carriage with horse and load   37½
- for man and horse   12½
- a person   6
- each horse, ox or cow   6
- each sheep or swine   2

As to how the Ashtabula River and Conneaut Creek were crossed by users of South Ridge, present-day Route 84, we need turn to the story of John Metcalf, who in 1808 made a contract to carry the U.S. mail from Cleveland to Erie, Pennsylvania. "It is said that he sometimes waded, and sometimes even swam the swollen streams with the mail bags poised upon his head to keep it high above water," noted Reverend John Hall in his "Early History of Ashtabula Township."

With the arrival of stagecoach service in 1814, greater pressure was placed on the county's residents to provide improved roads and crossings. On March 16, 1814, the county board of commissioners appropriated what appeared to be the first such expenditures for bridges: fifty dollars on the "Ashtabula bridge on the Ridge Road" and another fifty dollars on a bridge "across the south bend of Conneaught in Salem."

These simple timber bridges would eventually give way to more complex structures, built to last far beyond the ten-year anticipated lifespan of a simple deck, stringer or corduroy bridge. Even as settlers to the Reserve contended with the pathetic infrastructure, builders in Pennsylvania and New England were raising what looked like barns set over the great creeks and rivers. In the course of the next two decades, those designs and engineering feats would migrate west and help transform both a landscape and an economy as the bridges helped open up the backwoods settlements to markets and further settlement.

TRUSSES AND BUILDERS

Very few counties presented greater obstacles to good roads than the beach and maple townships in Ashtabula County; and I venture to say, that, very few people in any country, have been burdened with a greater weight of mud.
–*Quintus F. Atkins, "Notes and Incidents Connected With the Early Settlement of Ashtabula County, Ohio"*

A perusal of the county commissioners' proceedings from the time of the board's inception in 1811 until construction of the first covered bridge in 1832 shows that there were numerous timber bridges being built to meet the demands of residents. But the first mention of a "covering" over one of these county-funded bridges is in the journal entry for July 4, 1835: "On the application of the inhabitants of Kingsville for bridge money for two Bridges, one near Dixon's and the other near Mitchell's Mill the Commissioners agree to pay the expense of a good covering for each of them after they shall be satisfied that the work is done and the collections made in the fall."

Even allowing for the fact that a dollar was worth a great deal more in 1815 than it would be nearly two hundred years later, there is no doubt that the kinds of bridges being built at that point in the county's history were crude and quite temporary in nature. Many of the bridge appropriations were for twenty dollars or less.

References can be found in the commissioners' journal of adding planking to existing crossings, most likely ones made of logs on top of a log crib and filled with rock from the streambed. A September 2, 1856 entry in the Ashtabula County Commissioners' Journal notes that the board ordered seven dollars be paid to Orson Grant of Trumbull Township to compensate him for adding "planking" to a bridge that stood near his home.

The entry suggests that Grant had only a few stringers or a crib of logs for a bridge. In that same meeting, the commissioners appropriated $15 to assist with a float bridge project across the Grand River, Rome Township. Also, a bridge west of Rock Creek over the Grand River received a $125 appropriation that day. The low price suggests that the bridge was not covered; it was probably a simple corduroy or wood-truss bridge without a covering. Vertically set logs usually served as the abutments and midpoint piers; hauling sandstone or limestone to a worksite would have added significantly to the cost. The use of logs for abutments also explains the frequent need to repair these bridges; logs were easily dislodged during a freshet, a heavy rain that swelled the creeks and rivers.

There are several instances of commissioners funding "float bridges," raft-like structures that could go with the flow in streams subject to heavy

Early wooden bridges were not covered but used wood trusses to carry the load. These bridges had a short life because of rot and susceptibility to flood damage. *Jefferson Historical Society.*

flooding. An 1856 entry notes that a float bridge was to be built across the Grand River in Rome Township; the bridge cost the county $15. A March 6, 1850 journal entry notes that a bridge in Ashtabula Harbor was to be built on scows. The Plank Road Company was to pay half of the cost, not to exceed a total of $1,100. Based on a review of the commissioners' record (the privately built Rock Creek bridge excepted), the county's share of $550 was its largest expenditure on a single highway bridge up to that point.

BARNS ACROSS THE STREAMS

Elsewhere in the eastern United States, bridge builders were beginning to cover their wooden bridges and test new design approaches to achieve longer, stronger structures. Eric Sloane, in his *American Barns and Covered Bridges*, wrote that a partially roofed bridge was built over the Mohawk River in 1810, although the roofing and siding did not come until 1825–30. An unverified construction date of 1789 for the Carleton Bridge in Swanzey, New Hampshire, sets that bridge as the nation's first. Philadelphia claims that a Thirtieth Street bridge became the nation's first covered bridge when it was raised over the Schuylkill River in the early 1800s.

At the heart of any covered bridge is the truss, which supports the weight of the bridge and the load. The truss is based on the triangle, which cannot be distorted by stress (the downward pressure on the structure). There are typically two long and usually straight members called chords that run from end to end at the top and bottom of the bridge. The triangles of the trusses connect to these chords, and the unit works together to distribute stress throughout the structure. Because the trusses (each side of the bridge is one truss) hold the whole thing together, the integrity of the bridge depends on protecting those members from rot and damage.

The most basic of the bridge trusses is the kingpost: a vertical upright with two diagonal members, each one terminating at an opposite end of the chord, or lower member of the bridge.

The length of a single kingpost bridge is dictated by the length of the diagonal members of the truss. Single-kingpost bridges usually topped out at thirty-five feet in length. For longer lengths, builders simply added more "panels" or kingposts; collectively, these panels formed the truss of the bridge. Miriam Wood, in her book *The Covered Bridges of Ohio*, noted that Ohio bridge builders charged with the task of crossing smaller streams and canals built half-height (or pony) trusses, using the kingpost design, and covered only the sides.

Modifying the basic kingpost with the addition of a second vertical member and top chord creates the queen post design, which makes a span of up to seventy feet possible with a single panel. Variations on and combinations of these two designs were used by early bridge builders.

American bridge builders embraced the wooden covered bridge with gusto in the nineteenth century, building some ten thousand of them during the period between 1805 and 1880, according to the American Society of Civil Engineers. American bridge designers also attempted to outdo one another with truss designs that were more economical, efficient or conducive to longer spans.

Truss Designs

In 1805, East Coast bridge builder/designer Theodore Burr (1771–1822) obtained a patent for his "Burr arch" design that married the wooden truss and arch. American bridge builders were, at that point, still uncomfortable with committing a bridge's integrity entirely to trusses; thus, Burr treated the arch as the primary load-bearing element of his bridge. The ends of the arch were fitted into the face of the abutments, making for a very strong bridge. Burr arch/kingpost bridges also were expensive to build, however.

Sixteen years later, Ithiel Town (1784–1844) received a patent for his lattice bridge—aside from the simple king and queen posts, the first true truss design to act independently of any arch action. Town's lattice design used a series of forty-five-degree diagonal members attached to upper and lower chords with wooden pegs called "tree nails." These pegs, also known as trennels, were also used to connect the diagonal members at each point of intersection.

Town's design gave rural bridge builders an option that was much more economical than those requiring an arch. The diagonals were essentially common wooden planks that were relatively easy to saw on site or obtain from a nearby mill. The builder could easily adapt the design to a short span or, by using piers placed between the abutments, build a longer bridge in one continuous span.

Town was as much a businessman as a bridge designer, and he employed agents to inspect new bridges and collect the royalty of one dollar per lineal

Trusses and Builders

The diagonal planks of the Creek Road covered bridge create the unmistakable pattern of a Town lattice bridge. Bridge builders in Ashtabula County favored the design, which came with a one-dollar-per-foot royalty from its inventor, Ithiel Town. *Photo by author.*

foot. Considering that most bridge builders were charging nine or twelve dollars per foot to construct a bridge, the royalty added about 10 percent to the cost of a bridge.

As we shall see in the following chapters, Ashtabula County's bridge builders favored the Town lattice bridge over most other designs. The design's popularity was unusual for this region of the state. In July 1962, John A. Diehl, chairman of the Ohio Covered Bridge Committee, brought this distinction to the attention of Ross Smith, editor of Ashtabula's daily newspaper, the *Star-Beacon*:

> *Except for those in Ashtabula county and one in Sandusky county, which is living a very precarious existence, the Town Lattice covered bridge is really scarce in Ohio…I hope some way we can get a group in Ashtabula county to take one or two of the fine Town lattice bridges there under their wing to see that they are preserved. This sort of thing is being done in Preble, Montgomery, Muskingum, Scioto and Guernsey counties by local groups in the areas. They find that a covered bridge often attracts more indirect revenue than is spent keeping it in repair.*

Given that Ashtabula County had plenty of timber and water power, it is understandable why this design was so popular. Being made entirely of timber, a Town lattice bridge could be erected any place there was forest and muscle. Better still, if the stream was swift enough, a sawmill could be erected near the bridge site and thereby ease the burden. In Ashtabula County, bridge builders favored hemlock (trusses, typically) and oak (flooring). The Rock Creek twin bridge, for example, had white oak planks two and a half inches thick, ten inches wide and twenty-four feet long.

The approach to bridge erection has not changed appreciably; the truss was built on the stream bank or a heavy false work across the river. In the old days, block and tackle, winches and lots of muscle from men and beast either raised or pulled the completed truss into place. Then, as now, these "bridge raisings" were public.

The other design used in the county, especially on spans of 150 feet or more, was the Howe truss. Unlike the Town lattice bridge, the Howe truss depended on a supply of metal parts manufactured at a foundry, often in New England. It was not until railroads began to reach into the county in the early 1850s that these parts could be economically delivered.

William Howe introduced his covered bridge design in 1840, and it was an immediate success. Howe, a New Englander, improved on a design introduced by Colonel Stephen H. Long of the United States Army Topographical Engineers.[1] Whereas Long's bridge was entirely of wood, Howe introduced the concept of using wood for the truss's compression members and vertical iron rods threaded at each end for adjusting the tension.

As with Town's design, Howe truss bridges could be rapidly assembled and adjusted. However, the use of metal rods made the bridge more expensive to build. Suitable for longer spans, the truss bridges also found a devoted following among builders of railroad bridges. *The Covered Bridges of Ohio* notes that the railroads built hundreds of Howe truss bridges in Ohio alone.

One of these Howe truss bridges would figure prominently in the history of the county. While timber bridges of this design faithfully carried passenger traffic from 1860 to 1888 without a single death due to collapse, an all-metal Howe truss bridge over the Ashtabula River collapsed during a blizzard on December 29, 1876. More than ninety persons were killed in the crash and inferno that followed.

The press called the incident "The Ashtabula Horror," and with good reason. Nearly two dozen of the victims, including beloved hymn writer P.P. Bliss, were burned beyond identification. Further, locals looted the injured and dying of their personal effects. It was a night of shame and intense suffering, and the dark cloud lingered over Elias Howe, who was partner with his brother-in-law, Amasa Stone, in the Howe Bridge and Truss Company.

Stone had modified the wood-and-metal design for an all-iron bridge that used I-beams for the diagonal members. Civil engineer Joseph Tomlinson was hired to develop the bridge specifications and supervise construction. But Tomlinson resigned after Stone refused to reinforce diagonals that Tomlinson deemed inadequate for the task. Stone chose to supervise construction himself, confident that the bridge would be his career's crowning achievement.

A series of structural and construction errors followed, and while the bridge held together for eleven years,[2] news of its collapse did not surprise locomotive engineers who mistrusted it from the start. Stone ended up taking the brunt of blame for the tragedy, and he committed suicide on May 10, 1883. Howe's design, however, remained vindicated by the hundreds of other wood-and-iron bridges that performed exactly as engineered. More than 150 years later, three of those covered bridges still carry Ashtabula County traffic.

Builders

Commissioners' records and historical accounts are frustratingly silent on the subject of who built Ashtabula County's covered bridges. Unlike other sections of the state, which had prominent bridge-building contractors, Ashtabula County's bridge contracts appear to have gone to a variety of carpenters whose names history failed to record.

Robert Stewart

The exception was in the somewhat less glamorous but very necessary business of laying abutments, which was dominated by Robert Stewart of Kingsville Township. Although he lived in the northeast corner of the county, Stewart's livelihood was in the sandstone quarries of Windsor Township, in the county's southwest corner and on the Ashtabula/Geauga county line.

Three such quarries operated in the township during the 1800s. One at Windsor Mills, the Windsor Stone Company, was serviced by a narrow-gauge rail line that connected to the Baltimore & Ohio Railroad. It supplied stone to the Pittsburgh Stone Company. A quarry that supplied grindstone was located in Warner's Hollow on Grindstone Creek.

Stewart's quarry was in the northeastern section of the township, on Indian Creek, and supplied most of the stone used for bridge abutments in the county. The sandstone deposit was discovered on the farm of D.J. Alderman, and the vein was up to sixty feet deep; its quality was said to be better than that of the sandstone found in Berea, Ohio. The quarry started shipping stone in about 1870 and continued in business until about 1916.

Stewart, who worked as an independent contractor, was superintendent of the quarry. He depended on teams of horses to haul the stone to the various worksites in the county. Much of this stone traveled to construction sites on horse-drawn sleds; a typical stone weighed nine thousand pounds. Business was so brisk at Stewart's quarry that the hamlet of Stoneville—consisting of a few homes, a post office and a school—sprang up at the crossroads. The introduction of concrete quickly doomed the business.

Another source of abutment sandstone came from the Thompson "ledges" area of Geauga County. The abutments for the Harpersfield bridge are credited to that quarry. Patrick Sullivan was the stonecutter on that job, and his abutment work remains in place on the south side of the bridge.

As for the bridges themselves, history has dropped but a crumb here and there along the dusty paths that lead to the identity of their builders. The following list was compiled from research on the bridges and is no doubt incomplete, nor does it take into account the "modern" bridges, which will be dealt with separately in later chapters.

It is very likely that the task of building covered bridges was, at least in Ashtabula County, not a full-time occupation for any one carpenter but rather a matter of assembling a crew of workers skilled at building barns and structures of similar magnitude under the umbrella of a responsible party or "general contractor," in today's vernacular. Accordingly, both classes of "builders" will be addressed under this section.

T.S. Winship and Samuel Hayward

The July 18, 1867 entry in the Ashtabula County Commissioners' Journal notes that a contract was drawn up and signed between T.S. Winship, Samuel

Hayward and the commissioners for building a bridge across Ashtabula Creek in Kelloggsville (Monroe Township). Winship (1839–1892) was a Pierpont resident and merchant who had served in the Twenty-ninth Ohio Regiment during the Civil War. His mercantile affairs were conducted under the banner of Messieurs Smith and Haskins, but he chose Hayward for his bridge-building partner.

The fact that a merchant would get involved in building a bridge suggests that Winship and Hayward were general contractors who hired local men to do the work. The Williams Brothers' 1878 *History of Ashtabula County* mentions Hayward also being a partner in a cheese business.

In a letter published by the *Jefferson Gazette* newspaper on March 17, 1928, Volney H. Ormsby attributed the Gould covered bridge to T.S. Winship. Gould, a ghost town, was west of Pierpont. His letter gives insight as to how workers were called from other vocations to work on a bridge: "At the time the bridge was built [1873], my father and myself were running the old water saw mill located about 25 rods up the stream from the old bridge. In this mill we sawed a large quantity of lumber used in the construction of the bridge. When water was low so we could not run the mill, we worked on the bridge. We had no part in the contract."

Bentley

This name is mentioned in Miriam Wood's list of Ashtabula bridge builders. The most likely candidates are N. Bentley, who was thirty-five in the 1860 census, and J. Bentley, sixty-nine. Both were Lenox Township residents and listed their occupations as carpenter. Neither man's name appears in the 1870 census.

Potter Family

The surname of Potter appears frequently in biographies of the county's covered bridges, but writers have never stated a first name. It is likely that it was not just one Potter but rather several members of the Potter family.

Richard Potter, a Texas resident with familial ties to Ashtabula County, confirmed that his grandfather Louis Potter told him as much. He said that the Potters were assisted by other carpenters and farmers from the area, who hired on long enough to build a bridge.

Lemuel, who was born in Vermont in 1777, appears to be the most likely patriarch of this clan.[3] A general history of Madison Township, which broke away from Ashtabula County in 1811, noted that Lemuel Potter was a judge of the new township and that Samuel Potter was township clerk in 1811.

The Potters soon appear in census records of Harpersfield Township. The 1850 census places Lemuel and his wife, Polly, in that township but gives his occupation as butcher. That same census makes note of Samuel (Eliza), twenty-eight; Lansing (Hannah), thirty-four; and Orange (Sally), thirty-six, living in the township as well. All were farmers.

If indeed the Potters of Harpersfield Township were bridge builders, their greatest accomplishment still stands in that community. The Harpersfield bridge, which has been attributed to "a man named Potter" as well as "a man named Kreig," is the longest of the state's legacy bridges still standing and in service. Given the Potter family's long association with the Harpersfield area, it is reasonable to attribute this bridge to the Potter family, who perhaps received assistance from Krieg when the bridge was raised in 1868. Potter males residing in the township in 1870 and their ages at that time were Eugene, twenty-one; Olney, forty-two; Jabez, fifty-five; Homer, eighteen; Silas, nineteen; and Franklin, twenty-two. The latter three were the sons of Orange and Sally.

Potter is also credited with Olin's Bridge, built circa 1873. The Doyle Road bridge, while not directly attributed to Potter, is said to have been built by a "man from Vermont" who modeled the bridge after one in his hometown. This attribution fits Lemuel's heritage, but he would have been in his eighties when the bridge was built.

One interesting note about the Potter name is that it appears in the records of the Ashtabula County commissioners during the heyday of covered bridge construction in the county, but in conjunction with road study committees. An "O.R. Potter" was assigned to work with Calvin Dodge and Harvey Hill on the laying out of a road in Andover and Cherry Valley.

George Crowell and Samuel Ackley

Credited with building the double-lane bridge in Morgan Township over Rock Creek, Crowell and Ackley are said to have resided in nearby Rome Township.

Crowell, according to the 1850 census, was born in 1810 in Connecticut. His occupation at the time of the census was farmer. It is likely that George's parents had followed other members of the Crowell family from East

Haddam, Connecticut, to Rome Township. A William Crowell and his family were among the first settlers of the township, arriving from Connecticut in the fall of 1806.

Carpentry was in the Crowell family's blood. William promptly built a "house" for his family upon arriving in the wilderness, according to the Williams Brothers' *History of Ashtabula County*. In 1807, William Crowell erected the first log barn, twenty feet square, and the first frame barn in 1814. He assisted with the raising of the first log schoolhouse and the first frame house in May 1815. William Crowell Jr. worked on the joiner work for that building.

"William became a carpenter and joiner," notes the 1893 *Biographical History of Northeastern Ohio*. In the biography of Dwight Crowell, one of the eight children born to William and Nancy Crowell, the author writes that William "was one of the contractors to construct the Ashtabula and Warren Turnpike."

George Crowell, the son of Samuel Crowell, appears to have been a nephew of William's and thus likely to have grown up working with and learning from this skilled carpenter. Crowell would have been just twenty-two when he and Ackley tackled the task of building the bridge, so it is likely that William was, at the very least, working in the background as relative, joiner and contractor.

Samuel Ackley also was an early settler in Rome Township, arriving before 1828. Very little has been recorded of him or his family's history in Ashtabula County.

James H. Rogers

Born in New York, James H. Rogers lived in Sheffield Township, where he worked as a carpenter and joiner (1860, 1880 U.S. Census records). According to Howard Stanton, a longtime resident of Sheffield Township, Rogers was the head carpenter on the Benetka Road covered bridge, a Town lattice structure. Rogers, born in 1817, would have been about sixty years old about the time that bridge was constructed, according to an oral history of the bridge passed down from Stanton's grandfather, also a carpenter.

No official documentation of Rogers's involvement in the construction of any Ashtabula County bridge could be located, but Rogers certainly held the qualifications of a wooden bridge builder.

Seymour and Giddings

"The bridge over Ashtabula Creek, near what was formerly Young's mill, is also to be rebuilt and the abutments are to be put up by Mr. Stewart," noted a news story in the April 29, 1871 *Ashtabula Weekly Telegraph*. "The woodwork is to be of the lattice description, and the job has been taken by Messrs. Seymour, Giddings & Co. of this place at $11.50 per lineal foot. All parties to these jobs are capable, energetic and reliable men, and the work will not only be well done, but will be as speedily done as the nature of the case will allow."[4] As with T.S. Winship, this partnership appears to have been struck for the sake of acting as a general contractor and taking a profit from the job.

PRECIPITATING CIRCUMSTANCES

In the history of bridge building in Ashtabula County, there was nothing like a flood to get business flowing for the carpenters who either had to reassemble an existing bridge taken out by high water or replace an ill-conceived structure. The major floods that affected bridges in the county, as determined by a study of newspaper stories and advertising for bridge work, came in the following years.

September 1818

On September 24 of that year, commissioners appropriated $243 for repairing both bridges and roads, suggesting that flash flooding had washed out or damaged bridges and roads. The entries for that day and for March 13, 1819, suggest that the builder of a bridge across the Grand River was having a devil of a time getting the task done. After appropriating $30 in September, the board had to come up with another $75 six months later.

July 1837

A September 19, 1878 *Ashtabula News* article about "The Flood" noted that the Ashtabula River was higher than it had ever been known before, the prior record being set on the night of July 4, 1837, when it rose twelve feet in hours.

1857 (Multiple Floods)

Ashtabula Creek has been remarkably swollen by the recent rains. From observations taken last Thursday in Sheffield, it is known to have risen to within a few feet of the high water mark of 1837. Lumber to the amount of some 75,000 feet, owned by different individuals, has been swept away from the mills in Sheffield…serious damage has occurred to property of every kind along the creek.
—Ashtabula Sentinel, *June 18, 1857*

More than three months before this notice appeared, the county commissioners were dealing with the cost of repairing numerous bridges that were damaged by melting snow and rain. The bridge over Mills Creek in Austinburg had to be rebuilt at a cost of $100. The Plank Road Bridge at Ashtabula Harbor also required $100 in repairs. In Conneaut, five bridges required rebuilding—"at Browns Mills, at the Furnace, near Durkees and in Monroe near Wm. Tinkers and near Rathburns," reported the newspaper of March 4, 1857.

Another entry on that date noted that Hiram Lake saved plank and timber from the "center bridge" at Conneaut and was reimbursed seven dollars from the bridge fund for his trouble. In June of that year, the commissioners voted to set the rate of taxation for the bridge fund at six-tenths of one mill on the dollar valuation "including the amount necessary for the rebuilding of bridges destroyed by the late flood."

Bridge building in Ashtabula County almost came to halt four years thereafter as the Civil War began to drain male labor from the road and carpentry crews charged with the task of building and maintaining roads and bridges. Commissioners rarely appropriated money for infrastructure in those years, but starting in 1867, a decade of catch-up began. Bridges built during that period of expansion remain to this day.

1878

The flood last week was by far the greatest disaster to property that has ever happened in this county. Ashtabula creek was higher than ever before known; and the nearest approach to that height was on the night of July 4, 1837, when it rose 12 feet in 8 hours. On Friday last the flats [in the Ashtabula Gulf] were entirely covered by water, from town to harbor, and in the channel the current was eight to ten mile per hour. At the Harbor on Friday the scene was like Phillips' Napoleon, "grand, gloomy and peculiar."

Thus begins a lengthy article about the flood of 1878, which damaged or removed a number of covered and simple bridges in the county. The rain fell continuously for days, bloating the Grand River to a width of one mile in at least one spot. "Crooked creek, which passes through the southern part of [Trumbull Township], was large enough to float the largest boat that sails the Lake, and took off bridges and fences," reported the *Ashtabula News*.

So extensive was the damage from this flood, the commissioners called a special meeting on September 15, 1878, to raise the bridge tax by a half mill in order to fund the repairs.

March 1913

The statewide flood of 1913 has been called "Ohio's greatest weather disaster," and with good reason. No section of Ohio was spared when six to eleven inches of rain fell between March 23 and 27. The death toll was 467; more than fory-thousand homes were flooded. Bridge losses/damage in Ohio alone was more than $8 million.

Ashtabula County and its bridges were not spared. On March 25, the *Ashtabula Beacon* reported that Mr. Harvey and his family, who lived in the area of the Harpersfield covered bridge, had to relocate to the second story of their home. The *Geneva Free Press Times* of the following day reported that the family had a boat near their home just in case. And the entire community wondered if the 1873 covered bridge would succumb to the Grand River's maniacal fury. Even as the floodwaters receded, commissioners prepared to sell $75,000 in emergency flood bonds to meet the financial obligations resulting from the flood's damage to Ashtabula County's roads and bridges.

All across Ohio and the Midwest, covered bridges that were already being spoken of as "antiquated" crumbled under the surge of flooded

Trusses and Builders

The flood of 1913 nearly did in the Harpersfield covered bridge and did claim several of the county's timber bridges. *Todd Clark collection.*

rivers, their kind never to stand in that spot again. Further, by the time of the great flood, most counties already were opting for steel bridges.[5] The flood expedited the conversion.

During World War I, timber prices soared as the federal government tapped the forests for materiel. Civil engineers sought cheaper bridge-construction materials than wood. After the war, progress took its toll. Trucks became larger and capable of carrying loads much heavier than those bore by harvest wagons. Portals and rafters acquiesced to the indignity of a truck's tall cab or dump truck's elevated bed; floors and trusses sighed and collapsed under the load of steam tractors and overloaded trucks. Arsonists found the lonely bridges easy targets; in some cases, an hour's work settled any debate over replacement or rehabilitation.

It was as if the covered bridge had outstayed its welcome.

FORGOTTEN CROSSINGS

THE LOST BRIDGES

There are still remaining in Ashtabula County a large number of these highway overheads [covered bridges] *and most of them are in good condition. Engineers claim they will stand a twelve ton road roller or are good for any weight to which they may be subjected. These bridges are out of date however, and will never be rebuilt when once they were away, steel having replaced timber as building material.*
—Ashtabula Beacon, *July 19, 1913*

At least forty-eight historic highway covered bridges have been documented in Ashtabula County. In 1923, there were thirty-seven covered bridges in the county. By 1960, the number was sixteen.

A perusal of the records of the Ashtabula County Engineer's Office for the 1960s provides insights into why county engineers rarely mourned the passing of a covered bridge. In 1969, for example, the bottom chord of the Harpersfield bridge broke, and the truss had to be jacked up and a steel bent installed. A site in Mechanicsville suffered the same problem and received the same remedy. At the Benetka Road bridge, abutment repairs were required. And a truck too tall for the clearance ripped out the top bracing of Riverdale Road, requiring extensive repairs to the west end of the bridge.

Despite receiving necessary maintenance, the number of bridges continued to dwindle, until 1973, when just twelve remained. The stories of those bridges will be presented in the next chapter.

This chapter deals with the three dozen extinct covered bridges of the county, most of them "forgotten crossings" because they have been gone for so long that any remembrance of them exists only in photographs or writings.

The National Society for the Preservation of Covered Bridges, working with state historic bridge associations, assigns a unique number to each documented extinct covered bridge, as well as extant ones. The format is state-county-bridge: Ohio is state 35, and Ashtabula County is number 4. Throughout the remainder of this book, these numbers, along with the road location, will be used. Extinct bridges are grouped by the stream they crossed, starting with the Ashtabula River.

Ashtabula Main River Crossing, 35-04-50

From the earliest days of Ashtabula County's history, the ninety-foot-deep chasm of the Ashtabula River, which locals refer to as "the Gulf" or "Indian Trails Park," was a barrier to transportation and settlement. Further, flooding in the Gulf was a frequent event that damaged or destroyed whatever crossing could be built there. But a high-level crossing was beyond the community's coffers.

A steep, muddy "road" that hugged the sides of the chasm provided access to the "flats," the broad floodplain. The old road was roughly between Spring Street on the west side of the Gulf and East Fifty-first Street on the east side. This is sometimes referred to as Osborne Hill.

A second road, farther downstream, connected downtown's Main Avenue to Harmon Hill on the "East Village," present-day "Tannery Hill Road." Historian Walter Jack felt that there was evidence for an unnumbered covered bridge at Tannery Hill prior to the iron bridge that stood there when the 1878 flood ravaged the flats. A tollgate was located on the east, or Harmon's Hill, side of the bridge, suggesting that the bridge was a private endeavor.

This spot appears to have been the first place on the river where a bridge was attempted. A notice in the September 24, 1836 *Ashtabula Sentinel* encouraged residents of Ashtabula Township (east of the Gulf) to attend a meeting for the purpose of finding a means to erect a bridge across Ashtabula Creek near Harmon Mills.

It appears that there were at least three timber bridges at the previously mentioned "Osborne Hill." A notice in the *Sentinel* on January 6, 1849, sought bids for a new bridge because its predecessor had washed away in a

The Main Crossing bridge provided passage across the Ashtabula River for at least twenty years before the Spring Street overhead bridge was constructed, eliminating the need to descend the steep, rutted road to the valley. The ice floes are indicative of the kinds of threats the old bridge faced. *Author's collection.*

flood, the date of which was not noted. A third bridge was built in 1876 and was gone twenty years later. It was called the "Main River Crossing."

The bridge was severely damaged on February 3, 1883, when an ice jam broke loose and sent a wall of ice and water onto the flats. Timbers from the bridge creaked and submitted to the flow, but enough of the bridge remained to be rebuilt. It was obvious, however, that in order for the village and city to grow, a much safer and reliable method of bridging the Gulf was needed.

Even as the old covered bridge was patched up for another round of use and abuse, the debate began over where a high-level bridge would be built. A bond issue was approved by voters, and Lucius Jason Fargo, an east-side land owner with more than a casual interest in the development that would accompany a new bridge, donated the land to lay out what would become East Forty-sixth Street between the river's east bank and State Road.

Opened in 1896, the 1,000-foot-long, 110-foot-high Spring Street bridge quickly antiquated the Main Crossing. Nature reclaimed the rutted, muddy road, and the bridge was left to succumb to the next flood or ice jam.

CROOKED GULF, 35-04-01

Farther upstream, the Crooked Gulf bridge was higher above the river and thereby dodged many of the hazards faced by the Main Crossing bridge. Crooked Gulf, believed to have been a Town lattice structure, was built in 1867 and was 120 feet long.

In a newspaper article, Ashtabula County historian Alice Bliss recalled the bridge as a "tunnel" that seemed to terminate at a perpendicular wall of shale. The old bridge enhanced the ambiance of Indian Trails Park, and it was a favorite of photographers. Boys who relished the swimming holes under this bridge and the next two upstream (Blaine Road and Olin) referred to Crooked Gulf as the "First Bridge" of this triad.

The highway leading to this little paradise was steep and curvy, thus the "crooked" moniker. A covered bridge with an entrance on a ninety-degree curve was poor highway engineering, especially given the snowy, icy nature of the region's winters. Nevertheless, the bridge was reinforced with a support at midpoint in 1945 in order to extend its life and make it more accommodating to heavy loads. But just three years later, the bridge's demise was announced by the county engineer, and that same year, construction of a new iron bridge, parallel to the old bridge, got underway.

The Crooked Gulf bridge stood at the location where the Smolen-Gulf bridge now stands. *Dean Luce collection.*

The new bridge, which featured a modified approach angle to make travel safer for motorists, opened in 1949. The wooden bridge was dismantled after the new span was opened. The iron bridge served for fifty-five years, whereupon it was removed to accommodate construction of the nation's longest covered bridge some eighty feet above the old bridge site.

BLAINE ROAD, 35-04-02

At Blaine Road (Green Hill Road today), Plymouth Township, a covered bridge kept watch over the oxbow, a natural trap created by high banks and a U-shaped bend in the river. While Native Americans took advantage of the natural feature during their hunting expeditions to the area, the settlers found it an excellent location for mills. Samuel Amidon operated a sawmill at the site, according to an 1874 atlas. And, as was often the case in the progression of mills, a gristmill (owned by L.B. Howard) soon followed.

The Blaine Road covered bridge spanned the Ashtabula River in a scenic valley. Arson claimed the bridge in 1962. *Dean Luce collection.*

The Town lattice bridge was built in 1873 (some sources say 1862) and was 125 feet in length. Its clearance was 11 feet, four inches. Creek stone was used for the abutments, which rose 17 feet above the river.

Old-timers recall this area as Bobwood Valley. Halfway down the winding hill, a spring that had been used since pioneer days spewed its cool water for all who cared to partake.

As with the highway that led to Crooked Gulf, Blaine Road could be treacherous in the winter, and the bridge was eventually bypassed. But the covered bridge was maintained and used by local traffic. Its demise came in the early morning hours of July 15, 1962, at the hands of an arsonist.

"I was on the [Plymouth Fire Department] and my wife [Catherine] was a *Star-Beacon* reporter," the late Bob Ellsworth said in a 2009 interview for a newspaper story. "At the time we got down there, there was just one other truck there. I pulled off to the side of the road and told my wife, 'There's your picture.' I could see all the way through the bridge and every beam was on fire." His wife got out of the vehicle and lined up her camera, but the bridge was in the river before she could snap the image. "It just crumpled," Bob Ellsworth said.

The bridge was cherished by Bobwood Valley residents, as well as Plymouth Township residents in general. The arsonist was never apprehended; neighbors had heard some kids yelling and screaming in the valley earlier in the night, Bob Ellsworth said. "It was a shame. It was a decent bridge; it was still in use," he said.

GAGEVILLE, 35-04-30

The Gageville bridge was doomed by way of being on "the Pike," also called the "Road of Remembrance,"[6] State Route 170 and, most recently, SR 193. It spanned the Ashtabula River just north of the highway's intersection with Plymouth-Gageville Road.

The construction date of this bridge has not been determined, but a photograph from the early 1900s shows roof work being performed on the structure, suggesting that it had been there for at least a decade or longer.

A Town lattice structure, the bridge was disadvantaged by being on a major north–south road that linked Ashtabula County to the Youngstown area. A 1926 assessment of the structure, quoted in a Northern Ohio Covered Bridge Society quarterly in 1966, observed that the bridge was

The days of the Gageville covered bridge were limited when this photograph was made by Ned Luce in the late 1920s. A new bridge was being built alongside the old covered bridge, soon to be closed and removed. *Dean Luce collection.*

"not in good repair, over much trafficked brick highway about five miles off Buffalo-Cleveland Highway [Route 20], 1½ miles from Kingsville, South."

Photographs of the construction of the new highway bridge show that the old bridge continued to serve traffic during the construction period. It was mostly likely dismantled once the new bridge was completed. Its service ended in 1931.

KELLOGGSVILLE, 35-04-08

Farther upstream, the Kelloggsville covered bridge on Stanhope-Kelloggsville Road provided eighty years of service before it was replaced by a culvert.[7]

The Town lattice bridge, built in 1867, was seventy feet in length and fourteen feet in width. Commissioners signed a contract with Samuel

THE COVERED BRIDGES OF ASHTABULA COUNTY, OHIO

The Kelloggsville covered bridge, located on the Stanhope-Kelloggsville Road, was removed in the late 1940s and replaced with a large culvert. *Dean Luce collection.*

Hayward and T.S. Winship on July 18, 1867, for construction of the bridge, which stood south of the hamlet. The bridge was removed in 1947 after a culvert fifteen feet in diameter and eighty feet long was built under it. The culvert was said to be the longest in Ohio at that time.

This covered bridge had the distinction of being the only such documented structure on the Stanhope-Kelloggsville Road, formerly a privately developed and operated turnpike. Kelloggsville, at the northern end of the northside road, was founded in 1799. Construction of the fifteen-mile turnpike between Kelloggsville and Richmond Township gave the community a significant boost. Its builder, Caleb Blodgett, had the "corduroy road" built of logs covered with dirt.

Travelers were forced to ford the Ashtabula River at Kelloggsville, an issue Blodgett did not bother to address with a suitable bridge. Nevertheless, the turnpike builder cashed in on his road by constructing, in 1824, his Old Brick Tavern, which served the community and travelers alike as a meeting hall, tavern, school and dance hall. Teamsters traveling the turnpike tied up their animals in a lot next to the tavern and then slept on the floor of the barroom on blankets. The tavern was said to be so crowded at times that these teamsters had a difficult time even finding a spot on the floor—and this in a community that had fourteen hotels or taverns!

The coming of the railroads brought an end to this bustling community almost overnight. Both the road and Old Brick Tavern remain, however, long after the covered bridge gave way to a prosaic, albeit very large, culvert.

HILDOM ROAD, 35-04-10

A short distance off the Stanhope-Kellogsville Road and south of Kelloggsville, Hildom Road crosses the Ashtabula River in a lovely valley that lost its covered bridge in 1955.

The bridge was a Town lattice and a member of the class of 1867. It was seventy-five feet long, stout and well sited. When the devastating flood of September 1878 roared through this valley, the little Hildom Road bridge held its ground and emerged virtually unscathed.

The bridge was kept in good repair; a few years prior to its replacement with a structural steel bridge, the covered bridge received a new roof and

The Hildom Road bridge was set in a beautiful farming valley. Many of the residents of the area bemoaned the loss of the old but reliable Town lattice bridge. *Dean Luce collection.*

roof boards, new floor joists and reinforcements on one end. It appeared to be poised to serve the community for a few more decades, but County Engineer George V. Weatherston felt that a replacement was necessary.

"There is a touch of sadness in the passing of the Hildom Road covered bridge," noted an editorial in the May 5, 1955 *Star-Beacon*. "The replacement of the structure is a necessity, according to the hard-boiled realist. Again the quiet beauty of tradition must give way to the relentless march of progress. Only 20 such bridges now remain in Ashtabula County. Soon there will be none. At least one should be preserved as a memorial to that peaceful age of 100 years ago. It would serve as a reminder that it is possible to live—and live well—without the advantages of modern civilization."

Pierpont, 35-04-31

The East Branch of the Ashtabula River rises in seeps near the Pennsylvania border and flows northwest from there for twelve miles before joining the West Branch and forming the river's main stream.

Both branches and the main stream flow through farming country. In the settlement and development of this land, these streams presented a ready supply of moisture for farm animals grazing in pastures along their banks but also formed obstacles to the movement of products and people. Reliable but narrow Town lattice structures bridged these obstacles.

Three documented covered bridges stood along the East Branch; newspaper articles suggest that there could have been even more. After all, this little but troublesome stream intersects Turner, Hall, Marcy, Graham, Beckwith, Scribner and Adams Roads, as well as Route 7, also known as the "Center Road." Todd Clark has in his collection of covered bridge images a photograph purporting to be of a covered bridge on Beckwith Road that has not been recognized with a *World Guide* number.

The Pierpont covered bridge, 35-04-31, was one of three bridges on the Center Road that are referred to in newspaper articles from the 1870s. According to Alice Bliss's history of this bridge, the structure stood about a mile north of Pierpont and crossed the East Branch as it cuts a diagonal from the state line to confluence. The East Branch is a narrow stream, so a bridge of only fifty feet was required for the crossing north of Pierpont.

A postcard image of the Pierpont covered bridge is all that remains of the Town lattice structure. *Author's collection.*

The original construction of the bridge was sometime after July 24, 1867, which was when the commissioners advertised for bids to erect a fourteen-foot-wide bridge at the spot.

Walter Jack wrote that a flood prior to 1900 washed the bridge off its foundation, but it was repaired and restored to service. Looking at the narrow East Branch, it is hard to fathom the little stream possessing the fury and depth to remove a covered bridge. Then again, the flood that was responsible for dislocating the little bridge also unearthed and washed away an acre of potatoes owned by a Mr. Trimmer.

Adams Road, 35-04-11 and 35-04-47

Farther north, another covered bridge was erected across the East Branch in 1878, on Adams Road, Monroe Township. That bridge, 35-04-11, replaced another bridge, 35-04-47, which was built in 1868 and destroyed in the flood of 1878. The *Conneaut Reporter*, dated September 19, 1878, reported that two Monroe Township bridges, both near the farm of Charles Adams, were washed out. One of them was a covered structure.

There were two covered bridges at this location on Adams Road in Monroe Township. This bridge, 35-04-11, was built after the 1878 flood took out the first bridge. *Dean Luce collection.*

The reincarnation of this bridge had a 78-foot span and overall length of 103 feet. It was 12½ feet wide and had a portal 9½ feet tall. It stood at the north end of the road, near Scribner Road. The bridge enjoyed a relatively long life, succumbing to progress in 1947.

Adams Road is named for Charles Morris Adams, who was born in 1803 and died on April 20, 1888. Farms in the area around the bridge were owned by Adams's offspring.

Gould, 35-04-49

The Gould bridge spanned the Ashtabula River's West Branch. The little Town lattice bridge stood east of Stanhope-Kelloggsville Road in Pierpont Township and was built in 1873 by T.S. Winship. Its length was eighty-one feet.

Improvements to the Jefferson-Pierpont Road, present-day Route 167, changed the course of the road and left the Gould covered bridge

The Gould covered bridge and the community around it came to an end when a road relocation project skirted the hamlet. *Ashtabula County Covered Bridge Festival Committee collection.*

without a highway. The bridge was razed in 1927. The abutments were left in place and, along with the cemetery, are about all that remain of this community.

A March 13, 1928 article that appeared in the *Jefferson Gazette* reveals some details of the bridge: "For the past 60 years the old bridge has been on this spot where it spans the West Branch of the Ashtabula creek. Here the road took an abrupt turn past the old cemetery before it joined the [Stanhope-Kelloggsville] turnpike. This roundabout route has been abandoned with the advent of a generation that seeks the shortest distance between two points."

This article credits Johnson Ormsby and his son, Volney H., as carpenters on the bridge. Volney H. was still alive at the time the bridge was razed and provided more details of its construction. He told the reporter that his father owned a sawmill a short distance from the construction site. The mill used water power to drive an up-and-down, single-blade saw. A "vertical reciprocating motion was imparted by a crank after the manner of drag saw," noted the article.

Mr. Ormsby went on to note that this area along the creek was a huge producer of lumber, with fifteen sawmills standing "up and down the stream" between Steamburg, where the Sheldons had a lumber operation, and Phoenix, in northwest Pierpont Township. The Gould family laid the foundation of these mid-nineteenth-century enterprises that gave rise to stores and a post office at each location.

Steamburg, which was located in Denmark Township, was centered on the Sheldon Mill, which processed the high-quality timber that grew there. Grand schemes also grew in Steamburg, where a promoter by the name of Abel Meade plotted a town on the West Branch and spun wondrous stories of masted schooners docking at Steamburg, where a post office, a hotel and a church would be built.

The late Paul Hakala, who researched the subject of Steamburg, wrote that one family in Buffalo exchanged their valuable land for lots in the future metropolis on the West Branch. The sawmill departed after all the quality timber was sawed, and a number of investors in Steamburg were burned by Meade's scheme. Hope was revived when it appeared as if the Black Diamond Railroad would be built through the community and again when there was talk of a ship canal between Lake Erie and Pittsburgh. The proposed canal, which was never built, would have followed the West Branch through that portion of the county.

As for Gould, the loss of the mills and bridge doomed the little Pierpont Township community that once had four blacksmith shops, a store, a post office and a horse racetrack.

Conneaut Creek

Farnham Twin Bridges, 35-04-32 (south) and 35-04-33 (north)

Lovely Conneaut Creek once hosted some of the county's most beautiful covered bridges. The stream is born in Pennsylvania but soon enters Ohio, where it challenges north–south travel in the townships of Monroe and Kingsville, as well on the south and east sides of the city of Conneaut. The early settlers simply used the Lake Erie shoreline in order to avoid the rambling stream.

Ohio Route 7, which links Conneaut to Kinsman in Trumbull County, follows the route of an early road that was laid out after the War of 1812. It became a plank road in about 1840 and was outfitted with a timber viaduct at its first encounter with Conneaut Creek.

A tollgate was located on the north end of this structure, which evidently started out as a private venture. Ashtabula County commissioners took

The Twin Bridges of Farnham spanned Conneaut Creek and a millrace. *Olin Museum of Covered Bridges collection.*

responsibility for the bridge in 1858 and made the best of the situation during the Civil War. But because the viaduct was not covered, the timbers soon rotted and the bridge became too rickety for use. After the Civil War, there was a burst of bridge construction at Conneaut Creek crossings.

Among the extinct covered bridges of this stream, none was as famous as the twin bridges at Farnham, site of Fuller's Mill and a dam. The bridges were located in Conneaut near the border with Monroe Township. Because both the creek and a millrace had to be spanned at this point, two bridges were required on what was "Old Route 7."

The south bridge crossed the creek. Its construction came before the 1878 flood, which damaged the bridge at one end, according to the *Conneaut Reporter* of September 19, 1878. The masonry work on the bridge at the north end, which crossed the millrace, was severely damaged by the flood, and Robert Stewart was hired to rebuild it. Shortly thereafter, the bridge was covered. It is believed that the bridge was replaced in 1910 with another covered structure, a Howe truss.

The mill was built by a Mr. Jones sometime before 1825, but it was the partnership of Elisha Farnham and Thomas Gibson, Connecticut natives, that brought the sawmill and gristmill to prominence. They purchased the mills in 1830. Gibson dropped out of the partnership three years later, but Farnham persevered and in 1840 added a third mill. Farnham, who died in 1875, was involved in the Underground Railroad and was a friend of abolitionist lawmakers Benjamin Wade and Joshua Giddings.

The descent into Farnham was steep and dangerous and the bridges narrow, factors that eventually led to rerouting the road and eliminating the bridges. A newspaper story from 1926 noted that "the present bridges, commonly known as the 'Twin Bridges,' have been the scene of many serious accidents and at least one fatal, and are well known as a dangerous spot for traffic."

"The bridges also are old and will necessarily have to be replaced in several years. Both are extremely narrow, two vehicles barely being able to pass, and motorists, for the most part, prefer to wait until the road is clear rather than take a chance in such narrow quarters," concluded the newspaper commentary.

They were replaced in 1929 with a single-span, 150-foot concrete structure that cost $50,000. Because the dam presented an issue with construction of the bridge, state highway officials demanded that Fuller remove it. The mill itself burned in 1940, and the dangerous spot on Route 7 was eventually bypassed.

Mill Street, 35-04-29

Farther north, the Mill Street (Road) covered bridge stood on the creek's final loop around the city as it heads toward Lake Erie. Built in 1867, this Howe truss structure had a long history of being rebuilt and repaired. Wind damage suffered in the spring of 1924 ultimately doomed the bridge. Wind presents a significant load to a covered bridge, and that factor was sometimes overlooked during engineering. The bridge was determined to be unsafe, and it was replaced the following year with a handsome arched concrete span.

The covered bridge and road on which it stood took their name from the "Old Cider Mill" and, prior to that, the Rathbone and Skinner gristmill, both of which were located along the creek in this area. The cider mill was built in the late 1800s and survived until October 5, 1957, when it went up in a spectacular blaze.

The Mill Street (or Road) covered bridge in Conneaut was a long Howe truss bridge that was replaced by a concrete arch bridge. Several mills stood nearby the bridge. *Author's collection.*

Furnace Road, 35-04-07

Southeast of Conneaut, the Furnace Road bridge faithfully carried rural traffic from 1868 to 1950. A Howe truss bridge, it was 134 feet long and spanned 126 feet. Its width was 16 feet.

A March 8, 1866 *Conneaut Reporter* article noted that an old bridge at the site had been washed away by a flood; it does not specify the type of bridge that preceded the Howe truss structure, which had stone and concrete abutments.

Early industry demanded a stout crossing at this spot. Bog iron was discovered here circa 1830, an event that gave rise to a foundry a mile or so north of Clark's Corners (Furnace and Hatches Corners Roads). At one time, 150 men made stoves and other castings from the molten iron that flowed from the furnace of Furnace Road.

The covered bridge was handsome, set in a beautiful valley and approached by a curving road that delighted photographers. Those curves were removed when the new concrete-and-steel structure replaced the bridge in 1950.

The Furnace Road bridge was situated on a curving road on Conneaut's east side. The discovery of bog iron and subsequent construction of a furnace in this area gave the road its name. *Walter Jack, photographer.*

South Ridge, 35-04-51

West of Conneaut, in the hamlet of Kingsville, two covered bridges spanned Conneaut Creek, which flows south of the community.

Little is known of the South Ridge covered bridge, which was replaced by an iron span that has since been replaced with a steel-and-concrete span. Starting with Sherman's Mill in 1812, this valley hosted a number of mills, and the covered bridge's purported construction date of the 1820s fits nicely with the growth of industry there. The first woolen mill was built in 1820, followed by a second in 1830 and Matson's mill in 1837. If the construction date is valid, the bridge would predate the 1832 Rock Creek Covered Bridge.

The South Ridge Road bridge was gone by 1898.

The South Ridge bridge in Kingsville was one of two to cross Conneaut Creek in an area populated with mills. *Todd Clark collection.*

Kingsbury, 35-04-04

Upstream from the long-forgotten South Ridge bridge structure stood one that is much better documented. The Kingsbury Road (or Mill Road) covered bridge was built shortly before 1878, just in time for damage from the flood of that year. Alice Bliss wrote in her history of the county's covered bridges that the flood dislocated the Kingsbury structure from its foundation and caused much damage. It was repaired and returned to its abutments, where it would stand until the 1950s.

Photographs of the bridge suggest a Town lattice design. Length and other dimensions could not be located, but guessing from photographs, it appeared to be somewhere around 120 feet. This bridge crossed Conneaut Creek on Kingsbury Road, a dirt byway that still exists as two segments, one on each side of the stream. The land here is flat and subject to frequent flooding, but in the township's early history, it supported numerous ventures, including N.J. Kingsbury's flour and feed mill, which was located on the east side of the covered bridge.

The mills on these flats eventually gave way to a changing economy, flooding and time, reducing the need for a bridge in this corner of the community. The Benjamin Red Mill, which stood at South Ridge and the creek crossing, appears to have been the last to close, in the early 1930s.

Children cool off in Conneaut Creek near the Kingsbury bridge in Kingsville Township. *Walter Jack, photographer.*

By the mid-1940s, the Kingsbury Road bridge was no longer safe to cross and was closed. A photograph published in a newspaper on November 22, 1954, shows a picture of the bridge in which its entire roof and one side were badly damaged. Siding was missing. The caption stated that the creek had threatened to "spill the uneasy bridge into the stream" during a thunderstorm the previous summer.

A July 22, 1957 newspaper photograph showed the bridge still standing, one of nineteen remaining in the county. Shortly thereafter, the old structure buckled and collapsed into the creek.

State Road, 35-04-59

The construction date of this long-gone bridge is unknown. It was removed in 1898, but its abutments were used for its replacement and, in 1983, for the new covered bridge (35-04-58).

Grand River

Callender Road West, 35-04-49

Known as Callender Road West, to distinguish it from 35-04-24 over Rock Creek, the Town lattice bridge spanned the Grand River. The bridge's construction date is unknown.

It is known that the bridge succumbed to the Grand River's torrent in the 1913 flood. Five months after the flood, the Riverside Bridge Company began work on a new bridge of three spans. The steel bridge had a central span of 140 feet and two 50-foot approach spans, suggesting that the swollen river had cut a very wide channel or that the timber bridge was one of the longest in the county.

The flood actually gave the Callender Road bridge a new lease on life. The timbers were pulled from the river a mile or so downstream, and the bridge was hauled to Pierpont Township, where it was reassembled over the East Branch of the Ashtabula River. Thus was bridge 35-04-13, Graham Road, born (see next chapter for description).

Shaffer Road, 35-04-42

The Shaffer Road bridge also fell to that devastating flood that bloated the Grand River. It stood in Morgan Township at the site of the Shaffer Mill. The construction date of the bridge has been given as early as 1824, which if true would make it older than the double-barrel bridge that stood in Rock Creek.

The 1824 construction date is suspect on two counts. First, the bridge was apparently quite long, in the range of 150 feet, which would have been a very expensive project for a crossing in a remote corner of a fledgling township and county. Second, the mill at that location had not yet been built in 1824.

The first mills in that township were located along Rock Creek, according to the Williams Brothers' *History of Ashtabula County* (1878). Ambrose Humphrey built a gristmill there in 1808 and, six years later, sold out to Roger Foot, who also wanted to build a gristmill along the stream. The demand for millwork was great due to the influx of farmer settlers; indeed, there was so much wheat from Morgan, Rome, New Lyme and Lenox—all townships east of the Grand River—that came into the Rock Creek mill that the grain became "unsaleable" in the local market.

The Shaffer Road bridge in Morgan Township was lost to the flood of 1913. *Ashtabula County Covered Bridge Festival Committee collection.*

Foot and his son, also named Roger, decided that they needed to improve the quality of the flour being produced at their Rock Creek mill. In 1824, they traveled to Buffalo and Rochester to purchase the buhrstones and new bolting-cloth necessary to raise the quality of their flour. The mill was eventually fitted with the new equipment, and the flour produced by it, "upon being sent to New York, was surpassed by but one brand in market. It is said, also, that the first flour shipped to New York from [Ashtabula County] was shipped from this mill," noted the Williams Brothers' history of Morgan Township.

Foot ran into problems once the forest around Rock Creek was cleared and water flow patterns changed. That led Foot to build a mill especially adapted to low water on the Grand River. An April 17, 1913 *Ashtabula Beacon* story about the flood of that spring noted that water marks had been kept at the mill for seventy-one years. That dates the mill to at least 1842. Most mills required the service of a bridge, and it is likely that the Shaffer Road bridge came from that same era.

John Shaffer, born in 1813 in Braden, Germany, eventually came to own this mill, and the area around it became known as "Shafferville." Listed as a resident of Morgan Township and a "miller" in the 1850 census, this immigrant had the honor of a bridge, a dam, a mill, a hamlet and a road all bear his name.

The dam was a popular fishing spot and was the destination of a passenger steamboat that ran an excursion route between the Grand River bridge at Route 322 near Orwell and Shaffer's Mill.[8] These halcyon days came to an end with the flood of 1913. Harry W. Ray, who grew up around Shaffer's bridge and dam, recalled the flood in a letter to the editor published in the January 24, 1969 *Jefferson Gazette* newspaper: "Portions of the mill and bridge were lodged on Merry Isle, where the upper fork of Rock Creek enters Grand River, and remained there for years. The bridge was being replaced with an iron structure when another flood [in November] took it out and all had to be rebuilt."

The bridge that replaced the Shaffer covered bridge was 170 feet long and made of steel. Built by the Massillon Bridge and Structural Company of Massillon, Ohio, the iron bridge was 30 feet longer than any other steel bridge in the county when it was built in 1913. It cost $6,965.45, while the substructure cost $10,326.00. It is an eight-panel Pratt-through-truss design with riveted connections. A bridge of historic interest, it was rehabilitated in 2001.

Christy, 35-04-39

The Christy bridge, which stood on Johnson Road in Rome Township and spanned the Grand River, passed from the countryside without the drama of the Shaffer bridge's demise. Built in 1866, the bridge took its name from landowner James Christy, who owned four hundred acres of land and a sawmill on one side of the Grand River.

A stereoscope image of this bridge was made on July 3, 1886, and appeared in an *Ashtabula County Historical Society Quarterly Bulletin* in March 1968. The steel span that replaced the bridge was erected in 1905, so "Old Christy," despite its name, was a relatively young bridge when it succumbed to the forces.

Route 322, Orwell West, 35-04-37

A Howe truss bridge crossed the Grand River on Route 322 between Orwell and Windsor. It was built in 1884 and had a span of 112.3 feet and length of 116.5 feet. As was common along the Grand River in this area, this low spot was prone to flooding. A particularly severe flood in

1908 produced this story of thrilling escape filed in the Ashtabula County Historical Society's archives:

> *Windsor, Feb. 19, 1908—What might have proved their last ride was taken by Mr. Lepper and son last Saturday. These men are Bloomfield residents and had been to Windsor and were returning home by way of Orwell. Grand River was rising rapidly, and they were warned not to undertake going through the water, but they were determined to make the attempt, and on reaching a point just before the ascent to the bridge where the current was very swift, the horse fell.*
>
> *The men got into the water to assist the horse when they were overcome, and horse, buggy and men went over in the ditch against a wire fence. The horse got free and went with the current. George Cox of the New Hudson Road, a mile north of this road between Windsor and Orwell, was out on the river with a boat, getting muskrats, and coming near this part of the water, saw a man's hat floating, then he saw the horse's head.*
>
> *He came nearer and found the men clinging to the wire fence in an almost frozen condition. He got his boat close enough and got one man in, rowed out to the edge of the water and laid him down on the ground and went back and got the other one, took him out, then went to the house of Terry Fleming for a sled and help.*
>
> *The men were gotten to this hospital home as soon as possible, and Dr. Cannon [was] summoned, and their lives were saved. But for the timely and heroic aid of Mr. Cox, they soon would have perished.*

A steel span replaced the timber bridge in 1911, but that was not the end of its story. The bridge was moved to Fobes Road.

Fobes Road (Shaughum), 35-04-21

The relocation of the Orwell West bridge to Fobes Road[9] created a problem, however: The Howe truss bridge was too short for the span. It was 117 feet long, and the gap was 125 feet. The solution was to build an open deck bridge at one end. The entire project was done on the cheap: the extension was not covered, and wood poles were used to support both the covered and open bridge rather than stone or concrete abutments.

Forgotten Crossings

The Fobes Road bridge had a literal shortcoming: the bridge was too short for the span, and an addition had to be added to the bridge in order to make it serviceable on this Grand River crossing. It still had more than two decades of service left when Walter Jack made this image in the spring of 1945. *Walter Jack, photographer/estate.*

Alice Bliss described it as a "misplaced tree house," with its stilt-like supports. "When seen from the valley below, it has a weird and ungainly look as it stands so high above the stream bed," she wrote.

The bridge had a ten-foot, eleven-inch clearance. Its floor was made of two layers of planks, the top layer longitudinal. It was thirty-two feet from the floor to the streambed, making it one of the taller bridges over the Grand River. A photograph of the raging river in the flood of 1913 showed the waters up to the floor of the old bridge, which held despite being on wooden supports.

The remote bridge was never a top priority for maintenance, although it did receive a steel center-support pier sometime before 1960. The county engineer closed the bridge in 1963 because of its unsafe condition. The Northern Ohio Covered Bridge Society wrote to Ashtabula County commissioners and offered financial support to save the bridge, but there was evidently no interest on the commissioners' part. A Boy Scout troop likewise expressed interest in doing some restoration work, but no funding was available.

Its floor riddled with gaps that could swallow a pedestrian, its trusses leaning, guy wires strung to hold the bridge somewhat erect and much of its siding missing, the old bridge was a hazard that had to go. In the still evening air of early May 1971, fire was set to its timbers. The Morgan Fire Department officiated at the controlled burn.

About one hundred spectators were on hand, reported the *Star-Beacon* in a terse obituary on May 7, 1971. "The western section fell into the Grand River about 6:45 p.m. with the eastern section following an hour later."

Old Plank Road, 35-04-26

The Old Plank Road, made of lumber attached to log stringers, ran between Lake Erie and Pittsburgh, an incredible accomplishment, as well as testimony to the abundance of timber in the Western Reserve two centuries ago.

Although the namesake planks are long gone, the road's name remains in some sections of the region. In Windsor, it is also known as South Windsor Road and was home to this Town lattice bridge. The bridge crossed the Grand River near the Trumbull County line and three miles southwest of Orwell. In the pioneer road's heyday, a tollbooth once stood near the site of the bridge.

The Plank Road bridge in Windsor Township succumbed to arson. *Ashtabula County Engineer's Office collection.*

It was built in about 1870, the year a notice for bids was advertised in the *Geneva Times*. The span was 87.0 feet, the length 103.0 feet and the roadway 14.5 feet wide. It was set on abutments without a center pier. On one side of this bridge was a small steel span with arched sides that crossed a smaller channel.

This swampy area, just east of Fortney Road, was nicknamed "Frog Alley" and became a landing zone for African American families from the Cleveland area seeking cheap land on which to farm and build a homestead. Despite the frequent flooding that affects the area to this day, the old covered bridge's demise came from other sources.

In 1957, a newspaper article told of how large trucks were still squeezing through the low clearance of the bridge, just ten feet, eleven inches tall, the lowest of any covered bridge in the county. On at least one occasion, a motorist reported finding roof timbers in the road, evidently ripped out by a truck too large for the passage. The county highway department repaired the bridge, but its days were numbered—not by traffic, but by arsonists.

In June 1963, someone attempted to set the bridge on fire by igniting oil-soaked rags left in the middle of the floor. The fire was reported and no serious damage suffered. In 1969, the county highway department put a new roof and siding on the bridge, improved the approaches and straightened the frame. David Weir, who was county engineer at the time, declared that it was "probably the best covered bridge in the county."

In early September 1970, the bridge burned to the abutments in a 2:00 a.m. fire of suspicious origin. A strong odor of gasoline was reported by those first to respond to the scene.

A very small portion of this bridge had been preserved, however. When the renovation work was done in 1969, Weir had workers salvage the best timbers and siding and used them to construct a covered bridge interior along one wall of his office. That room has since been converted to storage, but at least a sliver of it lives on in an obscure corner of the Ashtabula County Courthouse Annex.

Rome Township Two-Lane, 35-04-45

In Rome Township, on Route 6, was the county's second two-lane bridge. This bridge has an unknown construction date, but it most likely came after the Rock Creek twin-lane structure. As with the Route 322 West bridge, the two-lane Rome Township bridge suffered from being built too low to the stream, which resulted in flooding. Newspaper accounts of the bridge's history quote neighbors who recalled seeing floodwaters engulf the bridge's deck. A man by the name of Vinton Way, who lived near the bridge, claimed that he once rowed a boat through the bridge. The water was so high that his head just cleared the rafters of the bridge's roof.

Alice Bliss, in her research on the bridge, determined that the north lane of the bridge was closed some years prior to the bridge being removed. A threshing machine that was too heavy for the structure damaged the planks on that side of the bridge, which was never repaired. As Route 6 developed as an important link to Cleveland, the tired, one-lane bridge simply could not keep up with progress, and it was removed circa 1930.

Cold Springs Road, 35-04-60

Very little in way of documentation exists concerning this Austinburg Township bridge. No construction date or removal date could be located. However, an image purporting to be that of the bridge exists. The 1874 map of Ashtabula County also shows a bridge at this location, which was a stone's throw from one of the springs that gave this road its name. A cheese factory stood near the crossing, and a school was to the west.

New Hudson Road, 35-04-40; Windsor, 35-04-27

The little New Hudson Road bridge started its life in Orwell, where it spanned the Grand River. Built in the 1870s, bridge 35-04-40 served at New Hudson Road until that location was chosen to test a new kind material for highway bridges: concrete. The Roman arch bridge built of concrete served very well but was doomed by its hazardous siting on curves.

The covered bridge was moved from New Hudson to Windsor Road in Orwell Township, where it was pressed into duty over Rock Creek. The bridge, 35-04-27, served there until about 1950, when it was removed in favor of a steel-and-concrete span.

Alice Bliss, in describing this bridge, noted that the area around Windsor Road where the bridge was relocated was known as "New England" to the residents.

MILL CREEK

Dorset, 35-04-36

Mill Creek, so named because of the plethora of mills that once stood along the central-county stream, also sported a number of bridges, a necessary amenity when hauling grain and lumber to the mills for processing.

In Dorset Township, a covered bridge stood near the hamlet of the same name, in the area of present-day Route 307 and Russell Road. Built in 1868, the bridge was doomed by a flaw that immediately spelled trouble for the old bridges when speedy motorcars began crossing them: The old "Road to Dorset" took a sharp turn as it approached the little bridge from the west. The combination of a narrow span and sharp turn created a scenario for accidents as gasoline-powered speed replaced the horse on the highway.

"Another Accident at Dorset Bridge" shouted the headline in an August 31, 1926 edition of the *Ashtabula Sentinel*: "The sharp turn at the west entrance of the Dorset covered bridge was the scene of another auto accident Sunday night shortly after ten o'clock. The 1918 Buick touring car owned by Roy Smith, of Russell St., Ashtabula, crashed into the railing, and Smith suffered internal injuries. Miller's ambulance was called, and

The Dorset covered bridge was doomed by way of its location on a sharp curve. The Town lattice bridge was removed in the late 1920s. *Ashtabula County Covered Bridge Festival Committee collection.*

the injured man was taken to the Ashtabula General Hospital. With Smith in the front seat was another man, who escaped injury."

In the summer of 1930, the little bridge was eliminated as a new steel-truss structure was built on the realigned highway. The new bridge cost about $25,000 and was built by the White Construction Company, which also had the contract to remove the old bridge.

"The construction will include a super-elevated curve to eliminate the sharp flat curve that has resulted in several auto accidents in the past few years," noted a March 11, 1930 article in the *Jefferson Gazette*. "Several years ago, a large touring car with several occupants failed to negotiate the curve, crashed through the guardrail, over the bank and into the creek. All escaped without serious injury."

A news brief in the July 18, 1878 *Ashtabula News* suggested that this bridge was known as the "Collins Bridge." The article reported that Mr. Whitney immersed (baptized) three believers at the bridge. A cemetery near the bridge was known as the Collins Cemetery, and parcels to the south of the bridge and along Mill Creek were owned by J.S. Collins.

Forman Road (Eagleville), 35-04-17

The Forman Road bridge is one of possibly four covered bridges built in Ashtabula County during the Civil War. The Austinburg Township bridge is also known as the Eagleville bridge due to its proximity to the community.

The 1862 construction date was based on both a published advertisement for bids and a claim in an Ashtabula County Historical Society publication that the bridge's date was marked on the bridge. Where it was marked, however, was not disclosed. And the man who ended up dismantling the structure, Gary Hewitt, said that he never saw a date on any of the bridge's members.

There is written notice in the *Ashtabula Sentinel* of December 11, 1867, stating that commissioners would, on December 27, receive bids for construction of a lattice bridge at Eagleville over Mills Creek, as the stream was known at that time. Regardless of when the bridge was built, it did not stay at that location very long. In the spring of 1870, ice floes ground their way through the landscape around the bridge and cut a new channel about one hundred feet north of where the original span stood. The bridge had to be relocated to cross that channel and, in the process, lengthened.

The legendary flood of 1913 washed the bridge downstream, and with only horses and block and tackle, the bridge was returned to its stone abutments.

The Eagleville covered bridge stood on Forman Road. It found a new life as a pizza parlor after the county sold the bridge for five dollars. *Walter Jack, photographer.*

The county placed steel I-beams under it in 1963 and replaced the roof during that decade. But in 1972, the engineer's office determined that the bridge was unsafe and required replacement. County Engineer David L. Weir suggested the bridge be moved to the Ashtabula County Fairgrounds in Jefferson as a tribute to the bridges of the past. When that deal didn't materialize because of the high cost of rigging and moving, commissioners offered it to the highest bidder.

North Kingsville businessman Gary Hewitt had just opened his Covered Bridge Pizza Parlor in his hometown. His inspiration for the bridge-themed parlor was the clientele at a bar he owned in Kent, home to Kent State University. "We'd just gone through the 1970 riots at Kent, and the young people were trying to reach back; they thought the good-old days were better days," Hewitt said in an article published in 2009. He felt that the covered bridge was iconic of those "good old days," and he opened the pizza shop under that name with plans to eventually build a new structure with the architecture of a covered bridge. But when the county offered the Eagleville bridge at auction, Hewitt's plans were moved up a few years.

He jotted down "$5" on a piece of paper, slipped the paper into an envelope, sealed it and presented it to the board as the bid period was closing. "It so happened it was the only bid. Later that afternoon, they did have another bid from Cleveland, but it was too late," he said. "I was the proud owner of an 1862 bridge." Hewitt likes to tell people that if he'd known he would be the only bidder, he would have lowered his bid to one dollar.

With help from Glenn Bliss, Hewitt dismantled the bridge by hand. The shingles came off first, then the roof. When the Town lattice trusses were disassembled, Hewitt marked each one (L-1, R-1, L-2, R-2, etc.) and took photographs every step of the way.

The bridge came down during the summer of 1973. Hewitt had just ninety days to complete the task, done entirely with hammers, crowbars and an iron pin used to dislodge the wooden pegs. There were fourteen pegs in each row of latticework and eighty-four rows per side. The task of removing pins was made more difficult by the rainy weather; with the roof off, the pins got wet and swelled in the timbers.

Gary Hewitt purchased the Eagleville bridge for five dollars, dismantled it and used it as the basis for two pizza parlors in Ashtabula County. *Photo by author.*

Also complicating the work was the constant stream of visitors and, of all things, a scavenger hunt involving members of an antique auto club. The members had to find out the bridge's vertical clearance measurement, which was posted on signs over the portals. Hewitt finally just shouted "ten feet, three inches" every time a visitor pulled up.

"You heard a lot of the older people tell about going through with their horse and buggy, stopping in there with their girl or existing wife under the old covered bridge. We had people coming back to look for their initials that they'd carved in there during those days," Hewitt said.

Hewitt opened his new Covered Bridge Pizza Parlor in late 1975. The parlor uses half of the Eagleville covered bridge for the patron dining area. The other half of the bridge was used for his Andover pizza shop in the southeast corner of Ashtabula County.

The bridge, it may be figuratively stated, thus spans the entire county, from near Lake Erie to near Pymatuning Lake. In physical reality, it was 135 feet long and had a span of 108 feet, prior to division. It had abutments of stone and concrete and stood 23 feet above the streambed.

March Road, 35-04-15

The March Road bridge is also known as the Prim's Sawmill, Old Mill Road and Route 167 bridge. It was built in 1862 on the "Jefferson-Denmark Road." According to the August 27, 1862 bridge bid notice, it was to be built over "Grigg's Creek." And there it served for eighty-five years.

When a road-relocation project moved the crossing over Mill Creek upstream, the bridge became isolated and unnecessary. Photographs of the aged structure suggest that the state gave up on it years before it was removed in 1947—it and Harpersfield were the only two covered bridges that Ohio was responsible for at that time.

The Town lattice structure did not pass from the scene without a eulogy. Alice Bliss, in her research on the bridge, quoted W.T. Simmons, who was born in 1862 and was still around for the bridge's departure. He stated that his father operated a water-powered sawmill about 150 feet upstream from the bridge. A private bridge owned by Dennis Williams stood at the site of a steam sawmill about one mile upstream.

A flood whose waters rose to within inches of the floor of the relatively new covered bridge washed out the Williams bridge. The stage was set for excitement, and people started to gather at the covered bridge to see what

The March Road bridge was abandoned after the highway was rerouted around the structure, which crossed Mill Creek. *Dean Luce collection.*

damage would be inflicted by the rogue bridge—although it was hoped that the structure would fall apart or become lodged along its path rather than take out the vital bridge. Bliss completed the story:

> *Simmons said it did neither and his childish mind was so vividly impressed that he could still visualize it as it came down intact, riding Mill Creek's turbulent waters heading straight for the covered bridge and all felt their bridge was doomed. The framework of the Williams bridge struck the covered bridge broadside, smashing a hole in its side and then folded up and passed under the covered bridge in pieces. The only damage to the covered bridge was the three broken boards. The hole was never repaired, and through it, Simmons said he killed his first wild duck on April 3, 1885, getting it with one shot.*

Phelps Creek, Alderman School, 35-04-41

At the opposite side of the county, the Alderman School bridge lived a short but fulfilling life as it linked scholars to learning.

Alderman School was at the corner of Cox Road (north) and Route 322. The Elsworth Alderman family who lived in this section of the township had a daughter, Ada Alderman, who taught at the school that would be named after her. Ada, who died in 1927, has been called the "premier educator of Windsor."

Phelps Creek posed an obstacle to education and travel for students who lived to the north of the creek along what is today Huntley Road (formerly Killdeer Road). In 1867, two covered bridges were built across this stream—one at Wiswell Road, which still stands, and one on Cox Road.

The Cox Road span had a short life. By 1890, the bridge was closed to wagon traffic, but because it was an important conduit for students who attended Alderman School, it remained open to pedestrian travel. It had disappeared from the scene by 1895 and was replaced with a swinging footbridge. Alice Bliss wrote that youngsters who crossed the bridge treated it as a piece of playground equipment and made it swing back and forth. This action eventually weakened the bridge and rendered it unsafe for even the relatively light footprints of schoolchildren.

The youngsters paid dearly for their fun. With the bridge out of commission, they had to take the long route to school, a trip of several miles.

Pymatuning Creek, Wick, 35-04-34

The spot where the covered bridge once crossed Pymatuning Creek on Route 322 should be of interest to treasure hunters. According to a 1930 newspaper article, a diamond ring valued at $700 was lost at this crossing, in a community known as Wick. The Wick bridge stood between Hayes and Creek Roads in Wayne Township. Three tributaries converge to form Pymatuning Creek just a few hundred yards south of this site, a low wetlands.

According to Edythe Dillon, who was interviewed for Alice Bliss's 1960s series on the county's covered bridges, crossings over Pymatuning Creek were in short supply in Wayne Township's early years, thanks to this swampy obstacle.

One crossing, built in 1813, was on Underwood Road; the second was a ford a mile north of where the covered bridge later would stand. An early attempt to build a bridge at this spot met with only partial success—fourteen dollars was allocated from the county fund to build a structure of timbers and poles, but the approach from the west was not built until after the new bridge had rotted away.

THE COVERED BRIDGES OF ASHTABULA COUNTY, OHIO

The Wick bridge, in Wayne Township, crossed Pymatuning Creek. The bridge fared poorly in the age of the automobile and was removed after several vehicles crashed into it. *Todd Clark collection.*

Excavation from an old beaver dam eventually was used to cover logs buried in the muck and create a corduroy road on the west side. An opentruss bridge was built, the predecessor to the covered bridge.

Edythe Dillon dated the bridge to 1867 and identified its builder as "C. Bentley."[10] The bridge cost $1,000. While the bridge was under construction, a temporary bridge, built by the residents, was used. Alice Bliss shared this amusing story about the bridge in her newspaper article:

> *The story is told that one Saturday afternoon Fred Hart's father, Jerry Hart, then a boy of 15 or 16, started to Andover to get his father, David, who was doing some carpenter work there. Mr. Bentley refused to let him cross the temporary bridge* [to the north], *so Jerry had to turn his team around and go up the Hayes Road and go to Andover by the present Route 6. This disturbed David as he knew the preacher from West Williamsfield would have to use the bridge when he came to Wayne to preach on Sundays. He went down* [he lived in Wick] *and found a chain padlocked across the bridge's entrance. He took a 6-by-6* [inch] *timber from the new bridge and gave the padlock a couple of*

good licks and dropped the lock and chain into the middle of the creek. There was no further trouble.

Some sources date the Wick bridge to 1867; it was replaced with a steel-truss bridge in 1931, fourteen years after Route 322 (Route 15 at the time) was paved.

A newspaper article from the summer of 1930 noted that replacement of the bridge was a priority because an automobile had crashed through its side the month before. The story is one of epic misfortune, dramatically recorded in the article, published on July 29, 1930:

> *Mrs. J.P. Thompson, Titusville, Pa., was slightly injured, narrowly escaping death, a diamond set valued at $700 is lost, an automobile was burned, and a hole twenty feet by ten was torn in the covered bridge over the Pymatuning river near Wick Saturday evening as a result of an automobile accident.*
>
> *After striking the side of the bridge, Mrs. Thompson jumped from the car just as it burst into flames and plunged over the side, the front wheels resting in the river bottom.*
>
> *Mrs. Thompson had been in Cleveland to visit her sister in a hospital and was returning to her home in Titusville. Apparently losing control of the machine as she entered the bridge, the car struck the plank siding which is ten feet high, tearing a hole in the side of the old covered bridge nearly twenty feet long. The machine balanced on the edge, and as Mrs. Thompson leaped out of the machine, it burst into flames and plunged into the river. All but the front wheels of the machine, which were beneath the water, burned.*
>
> *Mrs. Thompson suffered slight cuts to the face and hands…A diamond, set in a ring which she was wearing, valued at $700, was lost.*

Temporary repairs were made to the structure until a new steel span could be built. The diamond ring was not recovered.

Rock Creek

Two-Lane Turnpike Bridge, 35-04-23

Ashtabula County's first documented covered bridge was built across Rock Creek, which gracefully descends a series of rock steps as it flows south of the

The Covered Bridges of Ashtabula County, Ohio

The double-lane covered bridge at Rock Creek, built in 1832, is the earliest documented covered bridge in Ashtabula County. It was on a turnpike and built with private investment. *Todd Clark collection.*

village that takes its name from the stream. The Ashtabula-Trumbull Turnpike, a privately funded road that linked Ashtabula to Warren in Trumbull County, was completed in 1820, but at Rock Creek, the crossing depended on a floating log bridge. The arrangement was not very reliable, and as mail and stagecoaches ran on this line, a more workable solution was needed.

Thus were Samuel Ackley and George Crowell hired to build a double-lane covered bridge across Rock Creek. To help pay for the investment, a toll was extracted; the gate was just north of the bridge.

The bridge, built of hemlock and oak, was 119 feet long, 24 feet wide and had an overhang of 11 feet, 5 inches. A center partition separated the two lanes—one 11 feet, 3 inches and the other 11 feet, 9 inches. The dual lanes were there for efficiency—the turnpike was a busy thoroughfare, and two lanes ensured orderly traffic flow of man and beast. The center partition helped keep animals on task as they moved through the tunnel.

The turnpike and bridge nurtured the village of Rock Creek. Horses on the four-horse stage line were changed out there and at Orwell, and travelers could find refreshment and rest in both villages.

The bridge became an icon for Rock Creek, and to this day, a mural in the center of the village rightly honors the structure, generally recognized as the first covered bridge in the county with a stone foundation. Numerous floods and ice jams threatened this venerable structure over the decades. In 1884, the flooding was severe—water rose to the second floor of houses north of the bridge. The bridge, then sixty-two years old, stood its ground.

A fire in 1924 also failed to bring it down. Much of the village's business district was destroyed; the bridge was spared, although the flames licked the north end and ignited the roof. It was repaired and stood for another twenty-four years.

The road, which became State Route 45, eventually became too busy and important for a relic to impede further growth. "The covered bridge doesn't allow some of the larger trucks to clear it," Rock Creek businessman Harry Miller told a reporter for the *Ashtabula Star-Beacon* in 1941. Miller insisted that the community needed a new bridge "because today's fast-moving vehicles make the bridge a dangerous roadway, especially in winter."

The Traveler's Club, a Rock Creek community group, launched a drive to preserve the old structure—if not in place then as the focal point of a community park. There also was talk of relocating it to the county fairgrounds. Neither plan worked, and in 1948, the county's first covered bridge was dismantled and replaced by a steel-truss bridge.

A native son of Rock Creek, E.T. Abbott became famous in the West for laying out bridges and railroads. In 1941, Abbott returned to his hometown and told a newspaper reporter that he had made a thorough examination of the bridge and found it to be in excellent condition, "well put together with wooden pegs…oak and hemlock wood used." He attributed the fine preservation to the design, which allowed the free circulation of air to all members.

Callender Road, 35-04-24

Known as the Callender Road East bridge, the range of construction dates for this charmer has been given from the 1860s to the early 1900s; it is possible that both could be correct, had an earlier bridge been replaced. The accepted date appears to be 1870, however, which is in line with the period of Howe truss bridge construction in the county.

The bridge was ninety-seven feet long and spanned just sixty feet, an unusually short distance for a Howe truss bridge.

As with its much more famous cousin, the little Callender Road bridge was a victim of progress, but of a different nature. The bridge was located

There were plans to save the Callender Road bridge when the construction of Roaming Rock Lake required the removal of the bridge, but the village of Roaming Shores could not make use of the structure and it was lost. *Ashtabula County Engineer's Office collection.*

in the path of the Roaming Rock Lake that would be created by building a dam across Rock Creek. With the certainty of the bridge's demise, the county offered the bridge for sale to the public. Roaming Rock Development purchased it for one dollar, and there was talk of relocating and thus preserving the bridge.

When the water in the new lake started to rise in late 1966, the bridge met a different fate. With the expense of moving the bridge far more than the association wanted to invest in it, the decision was made to set fire to it. The deed was made public in a newspaper story published on December 9, 1966. The story revealed that fire had consumed the bridge a week earlier.

Route 322, Orwell East, 35-04-38

One of the county's least documented bridges spanned Rock Creek in Orwell Township. Bridge 35-04-38 was located on what is present-day Route 322. Built in 1860, it was a Howe truss bridge. An Ashtabula County

A postcard documents the extent of flooding that occurred along Route 322 between Orwell and Colebrook Townships. The covered bridge over Rock Creek held its ground. *Todd Clark collection.*

Historical Society publication notes that the bridge was "removed sometime after 1913."

That "sometime" was most likely after 1927; a news article that appeared in a Jefferson newspaper on April 23, 1927, reported that commissioners were planning to build a new bridge on State Route 15, the predecessor to Route 322, over Rock Creek, east of Orwell.

TRUMBULL CREEK

East Trumbull, 35-04-20

The East Trumbull bridge stood on Mechanicsville Road over Trumbull Creek, a tributary of the Grand River.

Notice was given in the September 11, 1867 *Ashtabula Sentinel* of the commissioners' intention to build "a lattice Bridge, with 55 feet span, over Trumbull Creek in Trumbull." Somewhere along the line, the bridge almost doubled in length to one hundred feet and a span of seventy-five feet. It is likely that the flood of September 1878 widened the channel, requiring an

The East Trumbull bridge was "nearly wrecked" in 1878 as a result of the flooding on Trumbull Creek. It stood until 1950, despite numerous other mishaps. *Walter Jack, photographer.*

extension or rebuilding of the 1867 bridge. A report from Trumbull that was published in the *Ashtabula News* of September 16, 1878, noted that "the covered bridge at East Trumbull is nearly wrecked. The water took away part of the north abutment, and no doubt would have taken the bridge had it not been for the timely work of the people."

As with many of the old covered bridges located in farming country, the mechanization of agriculture brought devastating challenges. An "old-fashioned" steam engine fell through a section of the bridge's floor in 1898, according to local legend. The engine was hauling a wagon loaded with corn. Farmers in the region, not wanting to lose use of the bridge, came to the rescue, put a plank under the machine and thereby extricated it. The men worked together to repair the bridge before another heavy load could come along and finish it off.

The bridge would stand for another fifty-two years before it yielded to a new steel structure in September 1950.

Trumbull, 35-04-46

Very little documentation has been left behind about this bridge, which was built in 1867 and stood on what is now State Route 534. The bridge was of one span and was removed in 1924. According to an advertisement published on September 11, 1867, the bridge was to be lattice and of a fifty-five-foot span.

Whitman Creek, 35-04-35

The little bridge over Whitman Creek was unique as the only covered bridge built along the shore of Lake Erie in Ashtabula County.

Whitman Creek is a relatively small stream that meets Lake Erie at the boundary between North Kingsville Village and Ashtabula Township. Lakeshore erosion has greatly altered the course that the original "Lake Road" of the nineteenth century took as it traveled the shoreline. When the Whitman Creek bridge was constructed circa 1890 to replace another bridge, that shoreline was several hundred feet farther north than it is today—the old Lake Road is thus in the lake.

The little Whitman Creek bridge took a beating from truck traffic and lake waves. *Author's collection.*

The Whitman Creek bridge appears to have been a Town lattice structure and was quite short, judging by the two or three photographs that survive. The site around the bridge was a favorite for picnicking, swimming and fishing. Alice Bliss, who had a personal recollection of the bridge, wrote in her series on the county's covered bridges that the bridge "was not much to look at, and was but a short bridge to cross the small stream, which did not add to its appearance."

The bridge was no match for Lake Erie's constant aquatic licking and the arrival of heavy motorized vehicles. A truck driver rolled the dice on the bridge supporting the weight of his truck and lost. Both the bridge and vehicle suffered damage; the former was repaired, but in the early twentieth century, the bridge was removed and replaced by a steel-beam structure. That bridge, which was narrow and still too close to the lake, stands isolated from the highway, which was relocated farther south in 1953. A culvert was used to cross Whitman Creek as part of that project.

Whitman Creek and its tributaries drain about 6,000 acres. In the mid-1940s, the stream and about 250 adjoining acres were put under option by the state for a possible state park. An article in the *Star-Beacon* noted that "the stream and its tributaries wind through picturesque valleys, providing spots of natural beauty adaptable to camping and study of wild life, with the possibility of bridle paths and numerous picnic spots." The possibility of a small boat harbor and beaches at the site also made it attractive for development.

Chestnut Grove at Geneva-on-the-Lake won out over Whitman Creek, which remains an undeveloped recreational resource.

THE HONORED DOZEN

SAVING WHAT REMAINED

Remove not the old landmark...
—Proverbs 23:10

The burning of the Fobes Road bridge in 1971 brought the county's inventory of covered bridges to thirteen. Two years later, the Eagleville bridge was removed and, eventually, resurrected as two pizza parlors. But the era of burning or selling covered bridges because they were in the way of progress, too expensive to maintain or an easy arson target ended when Gary Hewitt hauled away the last stick of timber from Forman Road.

Some two decades earlier, John Smolen Jr., while working on his family's farm near Mill Creek, witnessed the end of another covered bridge—March Road, which collapsed into the creek.

"We'd be down to the pasture and pieces of that old covered bridge would come by as driftwood. That made me conscious of the covered bridges we had around here," Smolen said in a newspaper interview.

That consciousness translated into action years later, when Smolen became Ashtabula County engineer, an elected position. Smolen, with the blessing of county commissioners, embarked on a program to save the dozen legacy covered bridges in Ashtabula County and, eventually, build six new ones. It's no wonder that Smolen, who is retired from the county but works in the family engineering firm, is known by covered bridge fans as "Mr. Covered Bridge."

The Covered Bridges of Ashtabula County, Ohio

The Mechanicsville Road bridge was showing its age in the early 1980s, when Ashtabula County commissioners tackled the job of remodeling all of the county's covered bridges.

John Smolen saw a need to both preserve Ashtabula County's covered bridges and build new ones. He was photographed here at work in the Ashtabula County Engineer's Office in the late 1990s. *Photo by author.*

"When you say the words 'covered bridge,' I think any person in the county—as well as in the state and even the nation—thinks of John. His name is synonymous with covered bridges," said Betty Morrison, who was director of the Ashtabula County Covered Bridge Festival for more than two decades.

The Honored Dozen

While Smolen's interest in covered bridges is rooted in childhood memories of pasturing cattle near the Doyle Road covered bridge and ice skating under the Mill Creek's wooden spans, his advocacy goes far beyond nostalgia. Wooden covered bridges are practical, durable, low-maintenance alternatives to the steel-and-concrete spans typically found in northeast Ohio. A timber bridge costs substantially more than a concrete span initially, but with proper maintenance, its lifespan is much longer.

Smolen pointed out that there are one-thousand-year-old timber spans in Asia. "[Road] salt does not deteriorate wood like it does steel or concrete," Smolen said. "In fact, salt is a preservative for wood."

While John Smolen makes his living as an engineer, he's also one to appreciate the beauty and tourism benefits of the covered bridge. He used aesthetics as a selling point when he drafted and presented to commissioners his proposal to save the remaining twelve bridges in the county.

"We observed that the public did not want us to get rid of them," Smolen said. "The difficult task was how to strengthen the bridges without ruining their appearance."

In 1980, Smolen convinced county commissioners that the remaining historical covered bridges were worth the effort and expense of

The Root Road bridge was in bad shape and in need of many repairs by the late 1970s. *Photo by author.*

rehabilitation. Those that couldn't be upgraded to carry modern traffic should at least be preserved by bypassing or repurposing. The goals of the county engineer and commissioners were:

- completely rehabilitate one bridge a year;
- strengthen each covered bridge to carry tri-axle truck traffic;
- preserve each covered bridge to last indefinitely;
- earn a reputation for well-kept covered bridges;
- promote Ashtabula County covered bridges nationally as a tourist attraction.

In the ensuing years, each one of those twelve original bridges was preserved, in most cases using county resources and renovation crews. In the process, Smolen became an expert on restoring historical covered bridges, and his office often fielded calls from county engineers in other parts of the state and nation.

It is safe to say, therefore, that the twelve bridges in this chapter owe their existence to John Smolen Jr. Each bridge was rehabilitated as a result of the vision and dedication possessed by Smolen and funded by the county.

Benetka Road, 35-04-12

Sheffield Township's Benetka Road covered bridge is claimed by just about every person in that neighborhood as "their" covered bridge.

The late Paul and Rilla Jeanne Wing, who lived on the property to the south of the bridge for decades, called it their bridge, as does Marion Peck, who grew up at the south end of Benetka Road. "There is no bridge like my bridge," Marion said.

The road was named after her grandfather, James Benetka, a Slovakian immigrant. But the area on the Ashtabula River where the bridge stands was known as Clark's Mill long before the road was named. The gristmill at this spot was the largest of the flouring mills in Sheffield Township. The sawmill was built in 1829 and expanded to a flour mill in 1840. The mills were rebuilt in the 1880s, according to Catherine Ellsworth's history of the township.

It is likely that there was a bridge of some sort over the millrace and stream early into the mill's history. But as to when the existing bridge was

The Honored Dozen

The Benetka Road bridge is claimed by its neighbors along the Sheffield Township road. It has redwood siding, which further adds to its charm. *Photo by author.*

built, there is debate. Most sources cite a date of 1900, but Howard Stanton, who owns land along the river, noted that his grandfather, who grew up in the area, said that a platform bridge spanned the river until 1878. That is when a wagon loaded with wheat destined for the mill crashed through the deck of the bridge, necessitating investment in a new bridge.

The timing was bad, however, for that was the same year as the devastating September floods. A newspaper report of the flooding in Sheffield Township noted that two bridges along Ashtabula Creek suffered damage, including the bridge at Clark's Mill, which was "carried away wholly." Volunteers managed to salvage the bridge by pulling it back to the abutments using block and tackle.

Stanton said that his grandfather told him the bridge was built by mill owner Jim Rogers of Gageville. An *Ashtabula News* article of September 19, 1878, reported that James Rogers of Sheffield Township had his sawmill washed away by the flood and that he lost his blacksmith shop "with lots of

Clark's Mill stood next to the Benetka Road bridge. *Author's collection.*

tools," a financial loss upward of $1,200. It is possible that Rogers had set up that mill to cut the lumber for the new bridge, or that it was just one of the several mills in the township.

The 1880 census gives further credence to the attribution. James H. Rogers, sixty-three, listed his occupation as carpenter. Born in New York, Rogers was married to Rachel. "He made up most of the covered bridge in his shop over there," Stanton said. "He was an expert at it."

Volunteer labor was used to place the trusses, built on the banks of the stream, over the river. "He told them not to bring a saw, they wouldn't need it," Stanton said, referring to the quality of the Town truss's prefabrication using tree nails.

As Howard Stanton walked through his beloved bridge, he paused to examine the saw marks left behind on the planks that compose the Town lattice trusses. He said that circular saws created radial marks; vertical or sash saws, powered by a mill, left a distinctive mark that indicates an older construction date—1860 or earlier. Timbers with both kinds of marks on them can be found in the Benetka Road bridge, suggesting that it came apart at some point and required reconstruction with newer replacement timbers.

That theory lines up with another story he told, of a storm, the date of which he could not remember, that washed the bridge downstream.

The bridge became lodged against a huge maple tree; the structure was salvaged from there. Another story relating to that storm has one of the residents of the valley riding around on horseback and rescuing victims from their homes.

The county renovated the bridge in 1985. Prior to that work, the bridge rested on four cut-stone blocks, a more "modern" approach to abutments and suggestive of a later reconstruction date. The north abutment was replaced with concrete when the bridge was renovated in 1985; the south abutment was reinforced.

When Tim Wing, one of Paul and Jeanne's sons, heard that County Engineer John Smolen planned to renovate the old bridge, he offered to bring in a railroad car of rough-cut redwood from the West Coast. Wing, who was using redwood on his home-construction projects, offered the materials to the county at cost. The redwood has weathered and given the bridge a very distinctive color.

County workers performed the 1985 renovation, which included the addition of laminated arches for additional strength. The arch is nine inches wide, thirty-eight inches deep and constructed from one-inch yellow poplar.

The $50,000 renovation raised the bridge by three feet. Floor beams were replaced, and a new deck was installed over them. The curving south approach to the bridge, which creates a blind spot, was not changed with the renovation. Accordingly, locals who use the bridge beep their vehicle's horn to warn other users of their approach.

CREEK ROAD, 35-04-05

Rising 25 feet above the scenic Conneaut Creek, the Creek Road bridge is a Town lattice, single span of 112 feet and 125 total length.

Historians have not nailed down the construction date of this bridge, resorting to "around 1900" as the best guess. A bid announcement that appeared in the August 5, 1871 *Ashtabula Weekly Telegraph* suggests an earlier date—commissioners were seeking bids for the abutment of a new bridge over Conneaut Creek at Amboy.[11]

The bridge was closed in 1963 when an ice jam damaged the bridge's support. An iron center-span support was added, but it became a collection point for debris. During a 1994 rehabilitation, the center support received a wall-type pier that redirects the river's flow. According to John Smolen,

The Creek Road bridge crosses Conneaut Creek near Camp Peet. The wing wall and center pier support are designed to divert the water and debris. *Photo by author.*

adding the steel framework effectively distributes the midspan support and roughly quadruples the carrying ability of the "girder."[12]

The county spent about $50,000 on the 1994 renovation, which included replacement of the deck and lower structural timbers. New exterior siding was added as well. The revived bridge was opened to traffic in September 1995.

Camp Peet, a Scout camp established in the 1920s, borders the creek at this point and provides hiking trails along the scenic Conneaut Creek.

DOYLE ROAD, 35-04-16

Legend states that the Doyle Road covered bridge was built to look like one in the Vermont hometown of the carpenter who built it. Doyle Road is one of the several county bridges thus attributed to "Potter."

The Honored Dozen

The Doyle Road covered bridge spans Mill Creek. It is one of several bridges attributed to "Potter." *Photo by author.*

The bridge spans Mill Creek northwest of the village and is of Town lattice construction. It has an eighty-four-foot span and a ninety-four-foot overall length. Its most distinctive feature are the long, narrow windows on each side that expose the diamond-shaped lattice work and give approaching motorists a view of whatever conveyance is already in the bridge. This original architectural feature was preserved during the 1987 major rehabilitation performed by Ashtabula County Highway Department workers.

Working under the direction of John Smolen, employees added ninety-foot laminated arches that reinforce the existing trusses and enable the bridge to handle modern traffic loads. Along that line, the bridge, which sits on a sharp curve, was widened by five feet, which allows two-lane traffic. Other improvements added in 1987 included a new floor and roof. The project cost $60,000 for materials.

This bridge is sometimes referred to as the Mullen bridge, a reference to the E.L. Mullen farm associated with the structure in its early history. The Mullen farmhouse stood near the bridge, close enough to cause the structure to catch fire when the house burned in August 1941.

At the time, the Carl Lukas family was living in the house, which was owned by Clara Redmond. A strong wind blew the flames in the direction of the bridge, which was saved through the quick action of the Wade Hose Company.

Graham Road, 35-04-13

This Town lattice bridge is the only covered bridge in Ashtabula County not open to traffic. It rests on a foundation built by the Ashtabula County Engineer's Office in a field near the bridge's original site on Graham Road. The bridge is the centerpiece of an Ashtabula County Metropark.

This little bridge did a great deal of traveling in its lifetime. At the time of the 1913 flood, the bridge spanned the Grand River at Callender Road (35-04-49) in Rome Township. The flood washed out the structure and carried it one mile downstream. The timbers were collected and hauled to Pierpont Township, where a bridge was needed to span the East Branch of the Ashtabula River.

It was at that point in the story that Robert Benson's family got involved in the bridge's history. Robert's house overlooks the crossing, and since the early 1970s, he has been the relocated bridge's neighbor.

His grandfather Albert "A.D." Benson assembled the recycled bridge at its new location. Albert was assisted by his son-in-law, Herb Munger, who sawed the red beech planks for the flooring. He was paid twenty-six

John Benson's grandfather built the Graham Road bridge a few hundred yards from where John lives. The bridge was moved to land donated by John and his wife after the county decided that the bridge had to be replaced. *Photo by author.*

The Honored Dozen

dollars per one thousand feet of lumber, sawed two and a half inches thick and in sixteen-inch planks. "That made up the width of the bridge, just room for two horse and buggies to meet," Herb Munger said in a 1971 newspaper interview.

Herb also had the task of making the trennels for the Town lattice members. Each pin measured 8.00 inches long and was 1.25 inches wide. He used oak or hickory, which was cut into blocks 8.00 inches long. The blocks were driven through an iron throw to create the round shape.

Robert Benson, who was born in 1922, said that his grandfather died when he was very young, but the story of A.D.'s involvement in rebuilding the bridge is embedded in family history. Robert added that his grandfather ran into difficulty and had to call on the expertise of an unnamed veteran bridge builder, who pointed out that the novices had the truss planks upside down.

Robert, who has lived on Graham Road since the late 1940s, said that the bridge was never strong enough to carry the loads farmers needed to haul across the stream. Back when he was a boy, there was a gravel pit operation near Route 7. If a team pulling a wagon full of gravel had to cross the

The Graham Road bridge is shown in a late 1920s image, when it was at its prior location over a branch of the Ashtabula River. *Dean Luce collection.*

stream, it would descend the hill on a spur and ford the East Branch rather than risk crossing the bridge with the heavy load.

He recalled the county testing the bridge's mettle annually and then posting the weight limit. The test was conducted with a dump truck loaded with stone that was slowly driven across the old bridge. "They'd watch and see how much the bridge sagged," Robert said.

By 1970, the old bridge had become seriously antiquated and was pegged for replacement. John Smolen, who was the county's bridge engineer at the time, said that the bridge suffered damage when a vehicle that was too tall for the portal attempted to enter it. An insurance settlement from that incident helped fund the relocation. "It was weak," Robert said of the covered bridge. "[The county engineer] had to restrict the height [of traffic entering it] with steel beams. It was under eight feet. Farmers were complaining about it."

The options were to move, burn or bypass it. Bob and his wife, Helen, didn't want to see it burned, so they offered to donate a portion of their land so the bridge would have a new home a stone's throw from the stream it faithfully crossed for nearly sixty years.

In the summer of 1971, cribbing was built under the bridge, which was raised onto rails and rollers. The bridge was rolled off its embankments and then moved to the new site using house-moving carts. The county laid eight pre-stressed beams sixty-six feet in length for the bridge's new foundation. Several years later, the bridge was rehabilitated by the county. The new siding and roof gave the old bridge a new lease on life as a picnic shelter and tourist attraction.

Because it is closed to traffic, the bridge has hosted a number of weddings, including a New Year's Day ceremony when the temperature was around zero. Bob assists with events at the bridge by running a power cord to the structure if electricity is needed. He also keeps the grass mowed and watches out for vandalism and other mishaps. "There was a fellow who parked up on top of the hill and pulled in so his truck was facing the bridge," Robert said. "He didn't put the truck in gear, and it rolled down the hill and hit the abutment [of the new bridge]."

Harpersfield, 35-04-19

The earliest reference to a bridge across the Grand River in Harpersfield was in the Connecticut Land Company's early survey papers. It was simply

The Honored Dozen

Built in 1868, the Harpersfield covered bridge is an Ashtabula County treasure that carries both traffic and pedestrians across the Grand River. *Photo by author.*

described as a "walking bridge." According to a history published by the Harpersfield Heritage Society, the first bridge built near the site of the present bridge was in 1814 by Josiah Dodge. When an ice jam on the river finally claimed that bridge in 1868, a covered bridge was built on abutments quarried at Nelson's Ledges in Geauga Township.

The replacement bridge was, until Smolen-Gulf, the longest in the state. The bridge is 228 feet long and has two equal spans of 114 feet each. The sturdy structure, which survived the great flood of 1913, is a Howe truss.[13] The 1913 flood cut a new channel for the river, and a 140-foot-long steel span had to be added to complete the crossing. An article in the August 11, 1913 *Ashtabula Beacon* noted that 10 feet had to be "cut off" the timber bridge in order to connect to the new steel bridge. A new pier and abutment were built as well as part of the work performed by B.F. Hewitt, contractor.

The road on which the Harpersfield bridge was built eventually became State Route 534, and as such it came under the care of Ohio's transportation department, which bypassed the bridge in 1959 and relinquished it to the county's care. Steel supports were added in 1957 and a new roof in the early 1960s after the old one collapsed under the weight of snow. The siding was replaced in the 1970s. In the early 1990s, the bridge was closed so both the steel and wood structures could be renovated. The steel bridge had extensive rust damage. Trusses were repaired, lower chords and rusted steel stringers were replaced and a new laminated deck was added.

John Smolen engineered the renovations, which would make the bridge strong enough for bus and emergency vehicle traffic. Two feet of additional height were created by suspending the floor beams below the chords. The deck, chords and floor were replaced. The renovation also involved adding a five-foot-wide pedestrian walkway to the west side of both the iron and covered bridges. Although not historically accurate, the walkway was necessary because the river bisects an Ashtabula County Metropark.

New siding with louvers was also part of the renovation, which was completed in 1992. The bridge was rededicated at the Covered Bridge Festival that year. With all the work that's been done to the bridge, only the trusses are original. The iron uprights that are part of the Howe truss design had to be replaced to accommodate the additional height of the 1991–92 renovation.

The Harpersfield and Wiswell Road bridges are the only two in the county listed on the National Register of Historic Places. Listed in 1975, Harpersfield was nominated by Miriam Wood of Columbus. In an interview several years ago, Wood said that she nominated it "because it was the longest such bridge still standing in Ohio. It is of the very sturdy Howe truss design and was a very important crossing of the Grand River when it was built in the late 1860s. It was a major improvement in transportation for the folks of this area."

The area surrounding the bridge was first developed by John Ransom, who harnessed the river to power a mill. The operation peaked in about 1843, when the gristmill, sawmill and woolen mills he owned employed thirty-five to forty workers.

Ransom built tenant houses and had a large company store, and the area became known as Ransomville. He sold his woolen mill to Aaron and Obid Blanchard in 1864. The new owners converted it to an axe handle factory. Fire claimed the factory and gristmill in 1877.

Caroline Ranson (1826–1910), daughter of John and Elizabeth Ransom, attended Grand River Academy in nearby Austinburg and was sponsored by Horace Greeley to study art with Thomas Hicks in New York City. By the end of the 1850s, Ransom was painting U.S. military generals and national politicians. Both Ransom's work and the town that bore her family name have fallen into obscurity.

MECHANICSVILLE, 35-04-18

The oldest of the extant covered bridges over the Grand River, this bridge also has the distinction of being the state's only Howe truss bridge with a Burr arch. It is a single 154-foot span bridge that has been bypassed but nevertheless continues to carry traffic. It is the longest single-span legacy bridge in the county.

Mechanicsville ties with the Wiswell Road bridge in Windsor for being the oldest in Ashtabula County. Both were built in 1867. The Mechanicsville bridge survived the floods, but the 1913 flood washed out the east approach and did significant damage to the west. The bridge was raised six feet in the process of restoring the roadway, just in case the Grand River ever rose to within lapping distance again.

The bridge was one of the last to be renovated under John Smolen's plan. The job was performed by Union Industrial Contractors from July 2003 to March 2004. The bridge was rededicated in May 2004 and opened to traffic, although a modern concrete span next to it carries travelers more interested in expediency than nostalgia.

The Mechanicsville Road bridge is a Howe truss with an arch. It was completely rehabilitated and offers travelers an alternative to the modern bridge. *Photo by author.*

After this bypass bridge was constructed, the old bridge was kept on life support until money became available for the ambitious and expensive task of renovation. The job cost slightly more than $540,000 and came from a Federal Transportation Enhancement Grant, with 20 percent local match.

Duane Urch was foreman on the job. In a 2004 interview for a newspaper story, Urch said that he had no idea how workers in 1867 were able to build the thing, given the tools available to them. "Everybody who worked on that job still hasn't figured out how they put this thing up," he said.

The old bridge was in bad shape when Union Industrial's team tackled the huge task. The span was bowed, and the northwest corner had dropped about four feet. One end of the arch was badly rotted and had to be rebuilt. Both the upper and lower chords, the continuous horizontal members of the bridge, had extensive decay.

Whenever possible, the original lumber was salvaged, but visitors to the bridge will notice that much of the lumber is laminated, a modern process that glues together several layers of chemically treated timber. "I was hoping it wasn't too far gone," Urch said in the interview. "There was quite a bit of existing material they wanted saved."

A platform was constructed under the bridge to make it safe for the workers, who tore off the siding, roof and roof trusses, cut out damaged bridge members and then rebuilt the structure, all without any kind of reference material to go by.[14] "There was a lot of physical labor, but everybody who was on the job thought it was one of the most unique jobs they had ever worked on," Urch said.

The two piers under the bridge were built in 1996 as a stopgap measure to stabilize the structure. They were left in place after the renovation because the bridge's weight actually helps keep the piers in place. The pressure counters the force of ice, floating trees and other debris carried along by the current.

Mechanicsville is in Austinburg Township and marks the spot of "the great crossing," an old ford that was used by Native Americans and French trappers. The builders of the Old Girdled Road chose this spot as the best place to ford the Grand River as well.

David Eldridge, a member of the second surveying party for the Connecticut Western Reserve, became the first man of European descent to die in the Western Reserve when he drowned on June 3, 1797, at this crossing. Eldridge, who was warned to not attempt a crossing, was fording the stream with his horse when he became entangled in the harness and drowned. His body was carried to Cleveland, where Eldridge became the first burial in that city.[15]

With a wide, shallow ford and deep water upstream, Mechanicsville became a busy community populated with a number of mills powered by the Grand. Ambrose Humphrey built the first gristmill at Mechanicsville in 1801; woolen, oil, saw and turning mills followed.

According to an oral history of this area given by Ella Francis Clark in 1929, the many mills of Mechanicsville went up in flames on a bitterly cold night in December 1874. The light from this conflagration was said to be so bright that residents of Madison Township, ten miles away, could read their watch dials by it.

The mill town never recovered from that fire, which evidently spared the covered bridge. Mechanicsville became a sleepy, hollow town populated largely by urbanites and retirees who own cottages on the Grand River.[16]

Middle Road, 35-04-06

The Middle Road bridge is located south of Conneaut a short distance from the Pennsylvania line. Built in 1868, this 152-foot-long Howe truss span became the subject of an emergency renovation in 1984 when its north end dropped 18 feet without warning in January of that year.

The bridge was closed, and Smolen feared that if snow were allowed to accumulate on its roof, the entire structure could collapse into the Conneaut Creek. The county's last "pure" Howe truss bridge was in danger of extinction. But Ashtabula County was in the grip of a recession that drove the unemployment rate to about 20 percent. Funds were tight, but Ashtabula County commissioners saw value in saving the bridge, and three volunteers—Robert Graf, Dean Horton and Guy Vorse—came forward. They were assisted by four paid college students and several county employees who, during 1984, saved the bridge as they worked under Smolen's supervision. Thanks to the volunteers, the entire project cost about $50,000.

Smolen, in an article he wrote for the Second Ohio Historic Inventory of Bridges, described the steps taken in shoring up and rehabilitating the bridge:

- STABILIZATION. Smolen used an ancient engineering principle to stabilize the bridge at the sagging end. A huge I-beam lever and fulcrum were built with used materials and seventeen tons of concrete counterweight to hold up the damaged end. Cribbing under the bridge was used to stabilize the structure during renovation.

The Covered Bridges of Ashtabula County, Ohio

The Middle Road bridge was rehabilitated by a crew of volunteers assisted by the Ashtabula County Engineer's Office. It is a Howe truss bridge and crosses Conneaut Creek. *Photo by author.*

- STRENGTHEN. As with all the bridge renovations Smolen tackled, a primary concern was making them strong enough for modern traffic, including ambulances and school buses. For Middle Road, Smolen's approach involved adding two wall-type concrete piers at quarter points. The piers are three feet into the bedrock. Their walls were filled by hauling concrete into the bridge in wheelbarrows and pouring it into the forms.

  Adding two piers also allowed Smolen to strengthen the long bridge with treated-timber laminated girders that stretch from the abutments to the piers. The bridge had sufficient floodwater clearance to place these girders below the bridge. The girders are 10.75 inches wide, 31.5 inches deep and 35.5 feet long. This approach also had the effect of changing the design of the bridge so that only the center span is technically a Howe truss; the laminated girders support the other half.

  The rehabilitation also included new floor beams, floor planking, strengthening the lower chords, replacing and enlarging the vertical tension rods and new shingles on the roof and siding on the entire bridge. The lower chords were upgraded with 3.5- by 11.0-inch southern yellow pine planks on each side of the chords. The vertical tension rods were upgraded with larger ones, and a laminated distribution beam was added to the center of the bridge for better wheel-load distribution. White oak was selected for the new floor system, which has 6.0- by 10.0-inch timbers and 4.0- by 10.0-inch floor planks.

In analyzing the bridge and its issues, Smolen noticed that the overhang on the eaves was insufficient. Combined with a list at the north end, water entered the bridge and dripped between the siding boards onto the lower chords. This caused the wood to rot. The renovation extended the eaves two feet to alleviate this problem. The ends were rebuilt in a Greek Revival style to add a touch of class to the bridge. While the bridge was given a new lease on life with this renovation, a sister iron bridge, which stood to the south of the covered bridge, was replaced with culverts.

A rededication and opening of this bridge were held during the county's first Covered Bridge Festival, October 13–14, 1984.

OLIN (DEWEY ROAD) BRIDGE, 35-04-03

When Barrie Bottorf speaks of the Olin covered bridge, it is always possessively, even though it is a county bridge. "It's our bridge," said Bottorf, who lives along the river downstream from the Plymouth Township bridge.

"It's an extension of our private property," added his niece Julie Grandbouche, who owns property on the east side.

"My entire life, that bridge was there and part of us," Bottorf said. The Town lattice bridge dates from 1873 and is 115 feet long. The venerated structure figured into the childhood of many a Plymouth and Kingsville township resident, as under it was one of the Ashtabula River's best swimming holes.

"In the old days, when I was kid, everybody swam under the bridge," Bottorf noted. "It was basically the community swimming hole. Upriver was another hole, where the boys swam—skinny dipping." The swimming hole was courtesy of a dam that has since disappeared. The deep hole underneath the bridge has filled in since Bottorf's childhood days.

Located in Plymouth Township, the Olin Bridge is named for the family who has owned property in this area for more than 150 years. Bottorf's familial connections to this land go back to at least 1850, when his grandfather Almon Olin was born in a log cabin on the west bank of the river. Almon's offspring

The Covered Bridges of Ashtabula County, Ohio

The Olin Bridge spans the Ashtabula River. The Olin Museum of Covered Bridges is nearby. *Photo by author.*

find it difficult to stray from this scenic section of the Ashtabula River. "Most of the property surrounding the bridge has been in the Olin family at one time or another," said Bottorf, who owns houses on both sides of the road.

Bottorf suspects yet another familial connection to this bridge. His grandfather was a stonemason, and he can't help but wonder if he didn't have a hand in constructing the original abutments of the bridge. "He would have been twenty-three at the time, and I can't help but believe he would have been involved in building the foundation abutment," Bottorf said.

The bridge is attributed to that mysterious carpenter named "Potter," and as with Potter's other projects, it proved durable and reliable. Nevertheless, by 1958, the Olin Bridge was sagging and required the addition of a steel center support. Four years later, someone tried to torch the Olin Bridge. "One of the neighbors came along and was able to put out the fire," Bottorf recalled. "If it had been another fifteen minutes, the bridge would have been gone."

By 1981, when Fred Bottorf died, the bridge's exterior really was showing its age. "A lot of the boards were missing, and the roof was leaking," Bottorf said. "When my father died, my aunt said, 'Why don't you take any [memorial] donations of money and fix up the bridge?' We thought that was a real good idea, and we did it."

The crew of nearly two dozen volunteers, many of them neighbors, whipped the bridge into shape in a matter of two weekends. They gave it a new roof, replaced siding boards, repaired gables, painted the ends and repaired/painted guardrails. When the work was done, County Engineer John Smolen presented them with a new sign for the bridge, one designating it as the Olin Bridge.

"It officially became the first covered bridge in Ashtabula County to be named after a family," Bottorf said. Four years later, the center steel support washed out, and a concrete wall support was built in its place. The concrete structures do a better job of diverting the water, thus preventing an accumulation of debris against the abutments and pier.

Six years later, John Smolen and his crew worked his renovation magic on the bridge. The bridge was closed to traffic, and lower and intermediate chords were replaced. It received new floor beams, planks and siding as well. When the bridge was rededicated at the Covered Bridge Festival in 1993, it bore little resemblance to the tired but quaint structure Bottorf walked through and swam under as a lad.

"I liked it better the old way," Bottorf said, with a hint of nostalgia.

RIVERDALE ROAD, 35-04-22

This Town lattice bridge is situated 31 feet above the Grand River, about 1.5 miles northeast of Rock Creek in Morgan Township. It takes its name from the road; there was a Riverdale community as well. The bridge is 140 feet long, spans 111 feet and rests on stone abutments. It is 12 feet, six inches wide and 10 feet, six inches in height.

Dating to 1874, the old bridge has a quiet history of faithfully crossing the Grand and serving as a community bulletin board. Undated photographs collected by Dennis Osborn for his documentation of the county's covered bridges show the bridge's portal plastered with advertising for Sherwin-Williams paints and other products/events. Circus posters and advertisements painted onto the sides of the truss members were also common in the "covered-bridge era" of our nation.

The Riverdale Road bridge, which is thirty-one feet above the creek bed, served in its original incarnation until 1945, when the county highway

The Covered Bridges of Ashtabula County, Ohio

The Riverdale Road bridge in Morgan Township is a Town lattice bridge with a steel center support. *Photo by author.*

department placed a steel support on a concrete foundation midpoint under the bridge. More extensive renovation came in 1981. The floor was rebuilt, and glue-laminated wood girders were added to the sides. This narrows the bridge slightly but has the effect of building a bridge within a bridge for additional strength. This approach also allows the bridge to be returned to its original state in the future, should purists so dictate.

In 1987, the bridge received a new concrete abutment for additional support.

Root Road, 35-04-09

Built in 1868, the Root Road bridge is 114 feet long and has a span of 94 feet over the West Branch of the Ashtabula River. Wind damage nearly did in this old bridge as it approached its 100th birthday. The bridge developed a strong list to the south; wires were attached to the structure and weight limits imposed to stabilize the bridge.

It survived another twenty years with these stopgap measures before undergoing extensive renovation in 1982–83. At the time it was tackled, the

THE HONORED DOZEN

The Root Road bridge, south of Kelloggsville, is a Town lattice bridge that crosses the Ashtabula River. *Photo by author.*

bridge was considered to be in worse shape than any other covered bridge in the county.

As with Riverdale, John Smolen cleverly strengthened it by building a bridge within the bridge using large laminated wood girders. This allowed the bridge to carry heavier loads with a minimal investment of labor; the former county engineer said that it is easier to install the girders from within rather than from below the bridge. The approach also provides the engineer with the ability to remove any sag in the structure. While these girders also could go underneath the bridge, on spans like Root Road, which is fairly close to the water's surface, the loss of floodwater clearance would be an issue. The downside of reinforcing a bridge like this is the loss of lateral clearance, which can make for a tight squeeze for wider vehicles.

The renovation project also involved raising the bridge eighteen inches, constructing one new concrete abutment and adding a new concrete pier at midspan. The bridge received new siding, guardrail, floor beams and flooring. The new floor beams, attached to the girders, provide additional support to the bridge as they are under the intermediate chords.

The bridge is located a stone's throw off Stanhope-Kelloggsville Road (see discussion of this turnpike under Kelloggsville bridge, page 44).

SOUTH DENMARK, 35-04-14

Crossing Mill Creek at a community once known as Williams Corners, this little bridge was, until construction of the Liberty Street bridge in 2011, the county's shortest at just eighty-one feet, with a seventy-six-foot span. The Town lattice structure was built at this location, South Denmark Road, in 1890.

Like several other covered bridges in the county, the bridge is said to have once stood elsewhere but was removed by flood and rebuilt over the stream. History has failed to record the original location of the bridge, if that is indeed its story.

As with the Dorset bridge, this little structure was inadequate for modern traffic, yet it managed to get by for decades. It was finally bypassed in 1975 by a more efficient two-lane crossing that improved the road/bridge alignment. The bridge was eventually renovated, and the work allowed it to be reopened to light traffic, although most people enjoy this little gem by parking at the end of the gravel road and walking through the structure.

The South Denmark Road bridge is captured on a bitterly cold night. The bridge has been bypassed but is open to traffic. *Photo by author.*

The Honored Dozen

Wiswell Road (Warner Hollow), 35-04-25

The Wiswell Road covered bridge, in Warner Hollow west of Windsor, towers above Phelps Creek on two piers. The bridge was built in 1867 and spans Phelps Creek. It is 120 feet length and has three spans.

The gorge, cut by Phelps Creek, is rocky, deep and heavily wooded, a favorite haunt for photographers and the Amish, who on Sundays frequently make a visit to the bridge the centerpiece of a family outing.

The bridge rests on sandstone abutments that were most likely cut from a nearby quarry. These abutments were modified and wing walls added during the extensive renovation completed by the county in 2004.

There are two piers, one of cut sandstone and another of concrete, that give the bridge additional strength. During the renovation that returned the bridge to full service, a fieldstone pier was replaced with one made of concrete and finished to look like sandstone. Ashtabula Construction performed the concrete phase of the work in 2002.

The bridge was closed to all but pedestrian traffic in 1971, when Wiswell Road was rerouted. But county engineers continued to maintain the bridge.

The Wiswell Road, or Warner Hollow bridge, is in Windsor Township. It towers above Phelps Creek on cut-stone abutments and two piers. *Photo by author.*

Funding eventually became available to reopen the formerly abandoned section of Wiswell Road, which was renamed Covered Bridge Lane. The rehabilitation project cost $250,000; the bridge was reopened in May 2004.

County highway department employees did much of the work over an eighteen-month period. Glue-laminated girders were added to the existing lattices to carry the dead load of the bridge, as well as live loads. Workers raised the bridge four feet, repaired the lattice trusses and added glue-laminated girders inside the trusses. Covered in yellow poplar siding, the bridge has a distinctive starburst design on the portals and four- by four-foot windows along the length of the structure.

This siding is 1.5 inches thick and 8.0 inches wide. Why so thick? In addition to durability, thick siding securely nailed to the bridge ensures that vandals won't be able to kick it off and steal the lumber, an issue with thinner siding used on previous renovations. In the old days, county bridge crews would stretch strong wire across the sides of bridges to deter this type of vandalism and lumber theft. The thicker boards and robust fasteners have proved a better solution. "Nobody is taking the siding off now," John Smolen commented at the completion of the project. "Not the way we are putting it on."

NEW CONSTRUCTION

JOHN SMOLEN JR. AND TIMBER BRIDGE REVIVAL

This thing [the State Road bridge] *has changed my life. I like my job and have wonderful, fond memories. I love going out there* [the bridge site] *every day. There is no substitute for accomplishment, you know, the work ethic. I like working with heavy timber.*
–John Smolen Jr., quoted in Western Reserve *magazine, 1983*

State Road, 35-04-58

Ashtabula County was gripped by recession and high unemployment in the early 1980s when County Engineer John Smolen looked to the past for a way to light the county's future. In 1983, Smolen led the effort that built over Conneaut Creek the first covered bridge to be constructed in Ohio since 1920, when wooden bridges were giving way to steel and concrete structures. The construction was in addition to his plan to rehabilitate the county's twelve historical bridges.

"It was a gigantic undertaking," Smolen recalled of the bridge rehab work. "It was one big project after another." Nevertheless, Smolen jumped on the opportunity to build a new timber bridge while funding and manpower were available to a county strapped for cash, jobs and bridges. "It was just something that needed to be done. Timber is good bridge-building material," he added. "It is lightweight and easy to work. I just had that desire to build a new covered bridge and the commissioners were eager to do it."

The Covered Bridges of Ashtabula County, Ohio

The State Road covered bridge in Monroe Township was the first new timber highway bridge to be built in Ohio since the 1920s. John Smolen led the project in 1983. *Photo by author.*

State Road in Monroe Township was chosen as the site for this honor. The bridge, which came with a $200,000 price tag, was made affordable by county commissioners' clever use of Comprehensive Employment Training Act (CETA) money. Commissioners Pete Iarocci, Harold Christian and Alfred Mackey submitted the project, which would bring a handful of temporary jobs to the distressed county while replacing an old steel bridge across the creek.[17]

Smolen, who designed the bridge, selected the Town lattice design. The timber resources were treated southern pine, whitewood and native oak (floor beams). It required ninety-seven thousand board feet of lumber. CETA paid $60,000 of the materials cost. Had CETA money not been available for construction, the bridge would have cost the county about $500,000.

The crossing required two spans of 70.0 feet each to create a bridge with a total length of just under 157.0 feet. It has a clear width of 17.5 feet and height of 14.5 feet.

The project ran into trouble early on when its manager got a better job offer and departed. Smolen had to pull double duty, working at the site and serving as county engineer. "I would go out to the site at 6:00 a.m. and stay with the crew until noon," he recalled. "I did that for the rest of the project."

New Construction

A crew of seven workers learned construction skills while earning paychecks as they built the bridge over a five-month period. One hundred inquiries were made for those seven positions.

Mark Mollick, twenty at the time, was unemployed and had an interest in carpentry when he applied for the job. "My father was a carpenter," Mollick said in a 2009 newspaper interview. "He taught me how to be a carpenter, but this was totally out of the realm of normal carpentry." He recalled the project as being like "a big Tinker Toy box. They built the deck first and built one wall on top of that and stood it up, then built the other wall and stood it up. We put the roof on and the ends on."

Mollick said that John Smolen explained every step of the construction and the engineering behind it. "That job taught me a lot. We did a little bit of everything on that job, operate heavy equipment, use every kind of tool you can imagine."

The bridge was constructed on one side of the gap, and for Mollick and the other workers, seeing their handiwork raised over the stream was the highlight of the job.

Set on machine rollers, the bridge was moved toward the first abutment and lined up with temporary I-beams set between the abutment and center pier. A winch truck provided by a house mover was used to get the bridge to the abutment, and then a crane in the river took over the work of positioning it onto the center pier and abutments. The midstream cement pier was built by county highway employees, who also resurfaced the abutments and ran the heavy equipment required for the construction.

The completed bridge was dedicated on November 6, 1983. It became the catalyst for the construction of five more new covered bridges in Ashtabula County as the Town lattice bridge design proved its adaptability and timelessness. Even more significant for Ashtabula County's tourism, the bridge firmly established the county as a serious contender for the state's covered bridges capital.

"It was like building a piece of history," Mollick said.

Caine Road, 35-04-61

Spanning the West Branch of the Ashtabula River, the Caine Road covered bridge was built in 1986 to mark the 175th anniversary of the county's political formation. The Pratt truss bridge was designed by John Smolen.

THE COVERED BRIDGES OF ASHTABULA COUNTY, OHIO

The Caine Road covered bridge in Pierpont Township marked the 175th birthday of the county and the first time a Pratt truss timber bridge had been built here. *Photo by author.*

As with the State Road bridge, construction was done on dry land, but with a twist.

"We cut the channel through and put the channel under the bridge," recalled the late Robert Ellsworth, who worked on the crew that built the bridge in 1986 and was interviewed by the author in 2009.

Visitors to the Pierpont Township bridge will notice a pond nearby. Ellsworth said that the far wall of that pond marks the bank of the river's former channel, which was rerouted under the bridge after the construction was completed.

The construction marked the first time a timber Pratt truss bridge was built in Ashtabula County. Thomas and Caleb Pratt patented this design in 1844. It uses a combination of vertical and diagonal members, similar to the Howe design, but in the Pratt approach, the diagonals slope toward the center of the bridge. Thus, the interior diagonals are under tension (balanced loading), while vertical elements are under compression. Pratt truss bridges were used extensively on railroad bridges, and a number of metal highway bridges of Pratt truss design were built in Ashtabula County. Smolen said that he chose the design because it provided a good balance of efficiency, cost and strength.

New Construction

A crane raises one of the trusses of the Caine Road covered bridge. *Photo by author.*

Unlike future bridges, which would be prefabricated from laminated timber, the Caine Road bridge was built on site, except for the roof trusses.

Ellsworth said that the Caine Road project started with just two workers, himself and another man, whose name he could not recall. The crew would swell to six carpenters as the work progressed. Walter Gryzan supervised the project. The first step in construction was to build a crib, on which the bridge would be built.

"We built the floor, then the north wall and the south wall [on top of the floor]," Ellsworth said. Cranes were brought in to raise the walls, starting with the south one. Ellsworth remembered the day well. "That evening, my father [Austin] died," Ellsworth noted. "He had been there [at the construction site] that day and watched us raise the first wall." Ellsworth added that the roof trusses were built off site. "Probably over to Jefferson. They were big, heavy things. John [Smolen] thought we were going to be able to push them around by hand, but we had to have a crane."

The roof of the bridge was originally oak shingles cut by members of the Ashtabula County Antique Engine Club. Ellsworth spent several days treating the oak blocks with antifreeze in an attempt to preserve the shingles that would be cut from the blocks. But the shingles failed and had to be replaced with modern materials in the mid-1990s. The Covered

Bridge Festival Committee donated $5,000 to the county engineer for the replacement project.

The bridge, which cost the county $150,000, was dedicated on October 12, 1986, at the Covered Bridge Festival. As part of the project, the approach to the bridge was made much straighter, but Ellsworth would have preferred that the engineer had left just a little curve in it so the beauty of the bridge's sides would be visible as motorists approach the portal.

GIDDINGS ROAD, 35-04-62

John Smolen selected the Pratt truss design for his third new timber bridge in Jefferson Township, Ashtabula County. Crossing the Mill Creek on Giddings Road, the 107-foot-long bridge was completed in 1995. The county received a federal highway grant of $427,000 to build the bridge. Smolen applied under a special section of the grant that allocated money for timber structures.

The Giddings Road bridge was painted white, a first for the county's modern timber bridges. It spans Mill Creek. *Photo by author.*

New Construction

Sentinel Structures of Peshtigo, Wisconsin, fabricated the laminated timbers, which were transported to the construction site on flatbed trailers and assembled by workers from BOG Construction of Berlin Center, Ohio, contractor for the job. The assembly took place in the winter and spring of 1995; concrete abutments were poured the prior autumn.

Erection of the bridge took place in May 1995, when two cranes rented from Midwest Equipment were brought on site to lift the two trusses, each one weighing forty-eight thousand pounds. The cranes "walked" the trusses from their construction site on the north side of Mill Creek to within reach of a two-hundred-ton crane. Workers attached a three-point boom to each truss and guided the erect truss over the gap.

Stanley Westfall had the honor of easing the trusses across the gap. "It's close quarters. Anything in close quarters can be tricky," Westfall told a reporter after wrapping up the task. He had but three inches of "elbow room" in which to work the trusses into place.

Once the east truss was in place, operators secured it with yet another crane on the south side and turned their attention to raising and setting the west truss. It took five hours to set the first one, but just three hours for the second. The entire bridge went together relatively quickly once the trusses were set and secured by several floor beams and roof trusses. The trusses were of yellow pine and the floor of oak.

The Giddings Road bridge has an opening 16 feet high and 22 feet wide.

Netcher Road, 35-04-63

The Netcher Road covered bridge crosses Mill Creek a short distance from South Denmark Road in Jefferson Township. The bridge was dedicated on August 29, 1999.

Designed by John Smolen, the bridge cost $819,050. It was funded with a Federal Intermodal Surface Transportation Efficiency Act grant.

Smolen chose the inverted Haupt truss design with arches for this charming bridge. Righter Construction of Columbus won the bid to construct the bridge, which was fabricated in Ripley, West Virginia, by Burke, Parsons, Bowlby.

Southern pine was used for the arches, walls, floor and roof and yellow poplar for the siding. Four cranes, one of them rated at two hundred tons, were used to position the twenty-four-ton trusses over Mill Creek.

The Covered Bridges of Ashtabula County, Ohio

The Netcher Road covered bridge is the county's only red covered bridge. Its architectural details are the work of the late Beverly Cowles; John Smolen was designer. *Photo by author.*

The bridge was stained red and trimmed in cream. The architectural highlights of the bridge include cupolas with copper roofs at each end. Its architecture, created by the late Beverly Cowles of Jefferson, has been described as neo-Victorian. It is 110 feet long, 22 feet wide and 14 feet, six inches tall.

Even as the Netcher Road bridge was being constructed, John Smolen was at work on his most ambitious timber bridge project for Ashtabula County, a multi-span structure across the Ashtabula River Gulf in the area where the Crooked Gulf covered bridge once stood. But the bridge that Smolen had in mind would span the Gulf at a height of nearly one hundred feet, allow for two lanes of traffic, have pedestrian walkways on both sides and be a fully functional highway bridge capable of carrying all legally loaded truck traffic.

Nearly a decade would pass before his bridge would span Indian Trails Park.

LONGEST, SHORTEST

This is a great honor to me. I couldn't ask for a better honor in my career.
—*John Smolen, upon the naming and dedication of the Smolen-Gulf Covered Bridge, August 26, 2008*

As John Smolen researched replacing an old steel bridge on the steep, winding State Road in Ashtabula and Plymouth Townships, he discovered that the route's traffic count was high enough to qualify a project for federal assistance. He drew up plans and went after the money, and after six years on the drawing board, construction of the bridge started under Smolen's successor, Tim Martin, in the summer of 2006.

"I knew it would be a landmark for the county," John Smolen said. "It was a deep valley, and [the bridge] would have to be high up and a longer span."

SMOLEN-GULF, 35-04-64

The 613-foot Pratt truss bridge over the Ashtabula River on State Road is the longest in the United States. It dethrones the Cornish-Windsor Bridge over the Connecticut River between Cornish, New Hampshire, and Windsor, Vermont. That bridge is 449.5 feet long. Purists, of course, will argue the point that the Smolen-Gulf Bridge is a modern structure built with modern techniques and equipment.

THE COVERED BRIDGES OF ASHTABULA COUNTY, OHIO

The Smolen-Gulf covered bridge, at 613 feet, is the nation's longest. *Photo by author.*

Designed for modern truck traffic, Smolen-Gulf could hold sixteen loaded semi-tractors lined up end to end on both sides and not wince. Smolen said that the fact that this bridge is on a busy highway—traffic count was about 2,500 vehicles every twenty-four hours—was key to obtaining funding. The project qualified for $5 million in federal bridge grants. The Ohio Public Works Commission kicked in $800,000, and the county's share of motor vehicle gas tax footed the balance of the $8 million price tag.

Finding someone to build the project was almost as challenging as assembling the funding. "No one has ever done this, and the odds of somebody building another one is pretty slim," observed Ryan Cochran, an owner of Union Industrial Contractors (UIC) of Ashtabula. "It is a very non-typical structure compared to just about any bridge we've ever built, and we've done some complicated projects," Cochran said in a 2008 interview.

Union Industrial won the bid to build the covered bridge—only one other firm was interested enough to place a bid. In contrast, Cochran said that there could be dozens of bidders on a concrete bridge project.

UIC's owners—Cochran, Dwayne Fisher and Cochran's sister, Kim Kidner, with input from their father and the company's cofounder,

Roger Cochran—talked it over and decided that the project was worth the gamble.

"We tend to be most successful with the jobs nobody wants," Ryan Cochran said. "The more difficult, the better our chances are for landing the project and being successful."

The owners had to write the book as they went along. It started with estimating the cost. There are no standard formulas once you get past the concrete and excavation work. The best UIC could do is get four or five of its most experienced people together in a room and come up with an estimate.

"Bidding this job was a huge risk," Cochran said. "If you could not do it the way you thought you could by looking at a piece of paper, it could basically shut you down tomorrow."

Safety was another big issue. The project would put carpenters and cement finishers in constant danger as they worked one hundred feet or more above the Gulf in inclement weather and against strong wind currents that rip through the valley.

UIC set a zero-tolerance policy for safety harness use. The unique configuration of the work required that it modify existing safety equipment to meet the needs of this job. Nothing was simple or off-the-shelf about this project.

The biggest challenge, however, was engineering the lift. Consisting of four equal spans of 152 feet each, the bridge would rise 93 feet above the Ashtabula River Gulf. Most covered bridges are only 20 or 30 feet above the water. While the two end spans could be built on the Gulf banks and rolled/pulled into place with cranes, the center spans—each one weighing 162 tons—would have to be lifted from the Gulf floor and eased onto the piers. The other option was to build them in place, a dangerous and expensive proposition, yet that's the way the old-timers would have done it, with a maze of false work some 90 feet high.

Construction got underway in August 2006 after all the environmental impact hurdles were jumped. To reduce the height of the bridge, shorten its length and make it a straight span, an embankment had to be created on the southeast side. For months, a steady stream of dump trucks hauled dirt excavated from the Plymouth Ridge Road property of Edwin and Debbie Friedstrom. Dirt from a cut made through the approach also provided fill for the embankment.

About 185,000 cubic yards of material were required to build the embankment, enough to create a five-acre, twenty-foot-deep lake on the Friedstroms' property. The work was performed by Koski Construction. In the Gulf, another 85,000 cubic yards of material were excavated for the footers and one thousand feet of piling driven into bedrock—up to sixty feet deep on the embankment side.

The three piers, three footers and two abutments required 1,800 cubic yards of concrete and 532,599 pounds of rebar to build. Once that phase was done, work on the bridge itself began on the Gulf floor and each bank.

The bridge was fabricated by Sentinel Structures in Peshtigo, Wisconsin. Its timbers are treated southern yellow pine. The wood is glue laminated and engineered to hold the heavy loads. Truss timbers were precut and drilled for assembly by carpenters, who worked throughout the fall of 2007 and winter of 2007–8 to build the four spans.

Tammy Vaux, a carpenter on the project, said that working on the bridge was unlike anything she'd done before because the scale was so large—timbers, nails, drill bits, bolts and hammers were all supersized for this massive project.

The builders had to strike a balance between preassembling as much of the bridge as possible while keeping the weight in check. They also had to construct the spans at a point that would be accessible to the cranes and still give the behemoths room to maneuver. "Make it too heavy, too far away, and all that work was for naught," Cochran observed.

Cochran and others on the UIC team did extensive research and constructed numerous scenarios of crane selection/placement, working angles/distances, lifting points and rolling options before bringing the cranes on site. They decided that, due to the tight quarters near the embankments, they would need to roll off the two end spans onto a steel platform so a crane down below could grab them and ease them into place. Smolen Engineering of Jefferson—the firm that John Smolen and his son, Andrew, started after the elder Smolen retired as county engineer—did the engineering work for those steel platforms.

They determined at least three cranes were needed for the moves. A three-hundred-ton lattice-boom crane would do most of the work. It was aided by a five-hundred-ton hydraulic boom crane and, when setting the end spans, a three-hundred-ton hydraulic. The lattice-boom crane was the most expensive to rent, and the lifts were planned to minimize their need for the unit, which cost $110,000, including $68,000 for delivery, setup and tear down. It arrived on sixteen flatbed trucks. The cranes were supplied by All-Crane in Cleveland.

Placing the cranes was critical. "You can put a three-hundred-ton crane in that river and not be able to pick up a pound because it's too far away," Cochran said. At most, they had a radius of only fifty feet from the center point of the crane to make their lifts.

The four trusses that make up the Smolen-Gulf bridge were lifted/rolled into place in May 2008. *Photo by author.*

The moments of truth came in May 2008. The stakes were high—loss of reputation, loss of time, loss of money and, very possibly, loss of life.

"If [a span fell], it would have been all over," Cochran noted. "If one span were to fall, that was probably $1.5 million, on the ground, broken, and we'd have to start all over. We're not big enough to say, 'No big deal.'"

Two days before the first lift was scheduled, a hard rain sent a torrent of water through the construction site and washed out the pad where the crane was to be situated. Crews quickly rebuilt the pad, and on May 6, the span on the north side was rolled into place. "Everything went into place like we thought it would," Cochran said. It took eleven hours.

With the first span in place, the iron platform was removed and reassembled on the southeast abutment for what would be the final move. The cranes were moved into place for lifting the center spans. On May 13, the first center span, at the north end, was lifted and set onto the piers. It took ten hours. Two days later, the second center span went up in just two hours. The final move, rolling the span off the south end and onto the abutment and pier, took ten hours to complete. It was done on May 28.

The lifts did more than affirm the thoroughness of the research and planning that went into the critical phase. They also bore testimony to the

Construction workers pause from their labor on the Smolen-Gulf covered bridge a few days before Union Industrial Contractors completed the structure. *Photo by author.*

workmanship of the tradesmen—each span had twelve holes that had to line up with twelve anchor bolts on the pier.

Throughout the late spring of 2008, roof trusses were raised into place while the cranes were available. Construction went rapidly once the spans were raised, as the massive floor deck sections were dropped into the spans and the pedestrian walkway inched across the Gulf on both sides. The galvanized steel roof sheets, 626 of them, went up starting in early July.

Meanwhile, the county did its approach work and prepared to pave the highway leading to America's crown jewel of the covered bridge world. Dedication was scheduled for August 26, at which time the bridge was officially named. The "Smolen" part obviously honors the designer and county engineer; the "Gulf" part is a nod to the heritage of the Crooked Gulf Covered Bridge, 35-04-01, which crossed the Ashtabula River at this point but at a much lower elevation.

The bridge is an American product—the wood is from Alabama and Arkansas, the concrete from northeast Ohio, the steel from U.S. mills and the rods manufactured in Painesville, Ohio. The builders came from Carpenters Local 95, Labor Local 245, Operators Local 18 and Brick Layers and Allied Trades Local 16.

Ryan Cochran doubts if there will ever again be a wooden bridge of this magnitude built in the United States. The construction costs are just too high, although the lifetime of the bridge should be much longer than a concrete span's due to road salt's preservative action on wood. One thing is for certain: for the several dozen laborers and tradesmen who worked on the structure, and the general contracting company, it's a great legacy to hand off to their children and grandchildren.

"I think for most of them, as good as it is, I think that after a few days on the job, it's just like any other job," Cochran said. "But when it's all said and done, they are going to have their notch in history. I hope they realize that as well as we do, that it is something special."

West Liberty Street, 35-04-P (65)

In early October 2007, Geneva city manager Jim Pearson announced a plan to build the nation's shortest covered bridge in his city. The bridge was to replace a crumbling crossing on West Liberty Street, a stone's throw from State Route 534. It would be just eighteen feet in length and use a single kingpost, the first modern kingpost timber bridge in the county.

Hailed as the cornerstone of a downtown revitalization plan, the bridge also would be a community effort, with native timber donated from the wood lots of Phil and Cathie Schmidt, William Gubanyar and Angelo DeVivo. Carpentry students from the Ashtabula County Joint Vocational School (A-Tech) signed on to fabricate the trusses in the school's shop and raise the structure over Cowles Creek.

Funding for the project came from the Ohio Public Works Commission in the form of a grant and loan. Pearson told city council members that concrete wall supports for the old bridge were sliding into the creek and that the structure had to be replaced. With the state funding, it made sense to construct a timber bridge at the site and create yet another tourist destination.

John Smolen designed the bridge, which does not have siding except for on the walls of the pedestrian walkways. Although a small bridge in length, it is designed to hold all legal road traffic. That required both a robust support beam and abutments. The latter were built by Ruben Schwartz Construction of Conneaut. Each abutment wall is three feet thick and ten feet tall. The walls are concrete reinforced with rebar, as are the three-foot-deep footers.

The Covered Bridges of Ashtabula County, Ohio

The West Liberty Street covered bridge, at just eighteen feet, is the shortest highway covered bridge in the nation. *Photo by author.*

"There is a semi-tractor load of rebar in those footers," Schwartz said in a newspaper interview. "I pity the guy who will have to tear that out. He will have nightmares with that."

The laminated main beam, forty feet long, was made by Sentinel Structures. Otherwise, the balance of the bridge is local timber. The vocational school took delivery of the donated lumber in early January 2010. Both poplar and oak were used.

After kiln drying, the wood was carefully cut and assembled into the trusses. An error in cutting or drilling would have set back the project, so a plywood template was built and clamped over each member before any drilling was done.

Students Mike Johnston, Bill Lago, Brandon McMurphy and Jordan Lynch were selected by carpentry instructor Jack McMurphy for this part of the work. He said that the four students showed a commitment to accuracy and detail. "The biggest thing about this is not to make any mistake that would require you to start all over," McMurphy said in a newspaper interview. "We can't go out and cut down another tree and wait to dry the lumber. We have very little room for error. Accuracy is a big thing with this, as is teamwork."

The side trusses are made of two-inch-thick oak boards, each one weighing about three hundred pounds. A sixteen-inch circular saw was required to cut the timber, and students used a three-fourths-inch, seventeen-inch-long drill bit to drill the holes for the bolts.

That work was completed in the early summer of 2010. The drilled and cut pieces were shipped to South Dakota, where they were pressure treated with copper salts and oil. That fall, students from the school began daily treks to the worksite, where the bridge was raised and completed during a period of several months. A crane was used to lift and place each of the trusses, which measure eighteen feet by sixteen feet, four inches and are fourteen inches thick. Each truss weighed four and a half tons prior to treatment.

A "tollbooth" stands at the east entrance and parking lot for the bridge, but no toll is collected. The booth is used to disseminate tourism literature.

The bridge was dedicated and opened during the 2011 Covered Bridge Festival. It marked an important milestone in the county's long journey toward becoming both a sanctuary for old timber bridges and a proving ground for modern ones. With eighteen covered bridges, all of them publicly accessible and all but one used for motorized traffic, Ashtabula County truly became the Covered Bridge Capital of Ohio.

MERELY A MENTION

Few there are who love a covered bridge until it is gone.

—unknown

RAILROAD BRIDGES

The scope of this book has been limited to highway and byway timber bridges, but the Society for the Preservation of Covered Bridges also recognizes and numbers railroad bridges with timber trusses.

There were nine timber railroad bridges in Ashtabula County, all of them gone. While several attempts were made to bring the railroads to Ashtabula County before 1850, it was the Lake Shore & Michigan Southern, of Ashtabula Train Disaster fame, that ran the first trains through the county. The obstacles were great. There were large chasms to cross at both Conneaut and Ashtabula. Both were bridged in 1852 using Howe truss spans—35-04-28 at Conneaut and 35-04-44 at Ashtabula. Additionally, the railroad built a 165-foot-long How truss over the Ashtabula River in the Harbor in 1880 (35-04-56) and, in 1877, constructed a 130-foot Howe truss (35-04-57) over a waterway referred to as "Stoney Creek."

The Pennsylvania Railroad built a 160-foot Howe truss (35-04-55) over Rock Creek in 1872; it was replaced with a 118-foot span (35-04-54) in 1880. That same year, the Mahoning Coal Railroad built a 130-foot Howe truss (35-04-43) over the Ashtabula River at a point south of town.

At Eagleville, the Pennsylvania crossed the Mill Creek with 120-foot Howe truss (35-04-52) built in 1872; it was replaced (35-04-53) in 1882. Both the Eagleville and Rock Creek crossings are on the Western Reserve Greenway Trail, which was created along the old rail line. Iron-truss bridges replaced the wood structures long ago.

Of all the wooden railroad bridges built in Ashtabula County, the most significant historically was the Lake Shore & Michigan Southern's Howe truss built in 1852 over the Ashtabula River (35-04-44). The wood bridge was replaced by the ill-fated metal bridge that collapsed in the blizzard on December 29, 1876.

The flood of 1878 appears to have been a seminal event for railroad bridge construction. According to the newspaper accounts of the flood, the LS&MS bridge at Ashtabula Harbor was washed away, and four bridges on the Ashtabula, Youngstown & Pittsburgh Railroad were lost.

It is unclear if these Howe truss bridges were actually covered; on the typical railroad bridge, the rails were on top of the uncovered trusses. There were instances of running the rails through a covered structure, like a highway bridge, but that created an additional fire hazard from cinders being spewed onto the wood, as well as the smoke and steam issues. In the days of wooden railroad bridges, an employee often stood by with a barrel of water at one end, ready to douse any small fires a passing train might have started.

Stringer Bridges

Several Ashtabula County property owners and businesses embrace their community's icon on private property. Nearly a dozen of these "stringer" bridges stand across drainage ditches and ponds for mostly decorative reasons. These little structures are recognized in the numbering system by a lowercase letter rather than a number.

Perhaps the most exceptional of these short spans is a thirty-two-foot Town lattice bridge that stands in Saybrook Township. It spans Indian Creek and was built in 1987 by David Oxley. According to his wife, Jeanne, David built the bridge as a retirement project. The couple moved to the North Ridge West property because Jeanne wanted horses. A stream of considerable flow after storms bisected the property; a May 1986 storm took out an iron bridge on the property.

David Oxley first built a scale model of the covered bridge that he intended to build across this stream, which flows into Indian Creek. During

Merely a Mention

David Oxley built this thirty-two-foot Town lattice bridge across a tributary of Indian Creek in 1987. The bridge is on the property that he and his wife, Jeanne, own on U.S. Route 20 in Saybrook Township. *Photo by author.*

the winter of 1986–87, he cut and drilled the timbers for his bridge, and with the help of family and friends, they built it over the stream in 1987.

The stringer has an interior clearance of seven feet, sufficient for a horse. Jeanne said that she had to teach the horses to trust the bridge before they would cross on it; the sound of their hooves on the deck spooked them at first.

Mentioned Bridges

During the research of this book, the author encountered numerous references to timber bridges for which there is no *World Guide to Covered Bridges* number. One explanation for these omissions is that they were not truly covered structures.

For example, the Tote Road bridge, remembered by some residents as a covered bridge, was actually two eighty-two-foot spans of steel supported midpoint by wood pilings. The wood pilings caught fire on September 28, causing the steel spans to drop into the river. The bridge, built in 1900, was never replaced.

The Laskey Road bridge across the Grand River was more likely to have been a timber-truss structure. The neglected bridge eventually fell into the river and was never replaced. The late Doreen Sutliff, in her history of Morgan Township, noted that loggers and farmers continued to use the failing structure after it had been condemned because it made a convenient crossing between Rome and Hartsgrove: "Many times they unhitched at the edge of the bridge, drove the teams across and then with long chains stretched back, hooked to the load and pulled that across…they did not dare put the full weight of teams and loads all on the bridge at the same time. Any use of it at all was at their own risk." The mention of horsepower being used to move crops across the bridge suggests that the structure was nearing the end of its life before the arrival of automobiles.

A history of Rome Township written by Christine Hiestan makes note of a covered bridge on Dodgeville Road that was replaced by a concrete span in 1910. The writer also referred to a covered bridge on Ketchum Road over Rock Creek.

A bridge referred to as "Gallagher" is documented in a photograph and has been assigned the number 35-04-O. The bridge spanned Shenango Creek at Simons, a ghost town that sleeps under the waters of Pymatuning Lake, which was created in the 1930s as a flood-control project.

Covered Bridge Festival

The first Ashtabula County Covered Bridge Festival was held on October 13 and 14, 1984. The centerpiece of this celebration was a birthday party for the rehabilitated Middle Road bridge. Participants received as a souvenir a small piece of scrap siding from the job.

The festival has been held every year since on the second full weekend of October. While based at the Ashtabula County Fairgrounds, the festival's events are spread out at covered bridge sites throughout the county. For more information, visit the festival's website at coveredbridgefestival.org.

Merely a Mention

Olin Museum of Covered Bridges

Barrie Bottorf's mother, Naomi (Olin) Bottorf, was known as the "Covered Bridge Lady" because of her birthright—she was born in a house next to the Dewey Road covered bridge—and her passion for that bridge and all covered bridges.

In her lifetime, Naomi Bottorf collected anything and everything related to covered bridges: postcards, sugar packets, soap, jewelry, placemats, paperweights, ashtrays, money clips, sun catchers, bells, magnets, puzzles, plates, pictures, newspaper clippings and hundreds of other items. She belonged to at least fifteen covered bridge societies and kept every newsletter they sent her. Her husband, Fred, who died in 1981, was likewise fascinated by the bridges and would carve their images into pieces of shale he found along the river.

When Naomi died in 1995 at the age of ninety-five, the family realized that this vast collection was material for a museum. Julie Grandbouche and her husband had inherited another aunt's house at the top of the hill east of the bridge, and they, along with Barrie's sister and brother-in-law, Holly and Brad Watson, decided to remodel the house and open therein the Olin Museum of Covered Bridges. At the time it opened, May 2003, the museum was the only one in the nation devoted to covered bridges, but just a few weeks later, the Bennington, Vermont covered bridge museum opened its doors. Since then, at least one other U.S. covered bridge museum has opened.

The museum, located at 1918 Dewey Road, Plymouth Township, is a natural extension of Olin Bridge, the museum's ultimate "exhibit." For hours and admission, visit the website at www.coveredbridgemuseum.org.

"Night Crossings"

Nighttime photographs of covered bridges are part of my "Night Crossings" project, a documentation of covered bridges using selective lighting and digital layering techniques.

Hours of setup are involved in making the photographs. I prefer working in winter, when there is snow on the ground and ice on the rivers. In addition to having a "blank canvas" that I can light and color as I see fit, the snow and ice ensures that I won't have to deal with mosquitoes and snakes.

The Covered Bridges of Ashtabula County, Ohio

I use a Nikon D800 body and, in most cases, a Nikkor 35mm f/1.4 G lens mounted on a Gitzo tripod. For lighting, I use the Paul C. Bluff Einsteins with wireless transmitters and a variety of reflectors. The strobes are powered by 110-volt lithium batteries. Each exposure typically requires five or more blasts of light from the strobe to build up sufficient exposure at the small apertures required by landscape photography. Typically, ten to twenty layers are produced for one image.

If I want a softer effect and the bridge is far enough away from light pollution, I will use an LED video light to slowly paint the bridge with the light beam during a long exposure. My favorite for this kind of work is the Comer 1800.

My work in the dark recesses of the county has generated more than one inquiry by law enforcement, a few minor injuries and many memories.

A gallery of my "Night Crossings" work, as well as an ongoing blog about Americana, history and photography, is at my website, http://thefeathercottage.com. I periodically add new images to my gallery of bridges from the Ohio/Pennsylvania/West Virginia region.

NOTES

Trusses and Builders

1. Long unsuccessfully claimed patent infringement against Howe but lost his case.
2. The railroad bridge that collapsed was, at the very least, the second to span this chasm. Some sources indicate that the original, wood bridge that opened in 1852 was 730 feet long. The county's other railroad bridge over the gulf, an iron trestle south of the LS&MS's bridge, did not come until 1882, when what was known as the Nickel Plate Railroad completed its line through the county.
3. *Memorial to Pioneer Women of the Western Reserve* tells of the tragic death of Polly's son, Chappell, who was killed by Frank Hartwell as Hartwell attempted to remove Polly from the house of her son, who cared for her in her old age. The death occurred in Harpersfield, where several Potter family members lived.
4. This appears to have been an advertisement for the Main Crossing bridge, 35-04-50. This is a rare instance of the linear foot price of an Ashtabula County covered bridge being documented in print.
5. Fairfield County was an exception. Miriam Wood, in her *Covered Bridges of Ohio*, noted that the commissioners of that county continued to fund covered bridge construction and that many of the county's wood bridges were built after 1900.

Forgotten Crossings

6. The road, between Youngstown and North Kingsville, was so designated to honor the fallen of World War I.

Notes

7. Culverts were in use on smaller streams long before this extreme example. An October 21, 1871 article in the *Ashtabula Weekly Telegraph* noted that a dilapidated bridge on the Plank Road, township unspecified, had been replaced by an arched culvert of three feet capacity and thirty feet length. D.I. Pratt was contractor.
8. Ezra Gregory of Harpersfield had a shipyard and landing on the Grand River, where he launched his boat *Gregory* in 1800. The thirty-five-foot-long boat provided merchants' supplies and commodities to settlers from Fairport Harbor in Lake County to Windsor Township in Ashtabula County. Similar boats operated from Austinburg and Windsor Townships, suggesting that the Grand River was much grander in its flow and depth than it is today. The boats provided a route into the wilderness for many new arrivals from New England.
9. This bridge was also called the Schaughum Bridge for unknown reasons. No such surname appears in Ashtabula County Census records. A 1946 news clipping noted that "the covered bridge over Grand River on the Schangrum Rd. in Morgan Township, which has been closed since May, was re-opened to travel this week." Adding to the confusion is that the New Hudson Road bridge, 35-04-40, has been called the "Shaughm bridge" as well.
10. The 1860 census makes note of an N. Bentley, thirty-five, and I. Bentley, both carpenters and living in New Lyme Township. A Lyman Bentley lived in Wayne Township but was involved in the cheese business.

The Honored Dozen

11. Amboy merged with Conneaut, as did Lakeville Village, the location of the Creek Road bridge, which would have been just south of Amboy.
12. Smolen noted that the Town lattice design offers engineers this flexibility of adding additional supports. He characterizes the Town lattice as an "open girder" rather than a true truss.
13. The Howe truss design usually incorporated metal truss support blocks, but the builder of the Harpersfield bridge substituted wooden blocks.
14. The siding from this bridge was saved and used on the interior of a barn at the Ashtabula County Historical Society's Blakeslee Log Cabin in Plymouth Township.
15. Eldridge's grave was originally in the area of East Ninth and Ontario; it was moved to Erie Street Cemetery when progress dictated that his grave be relocated.
16. Riverwood, a development of nearly four hundred acres "as cool, quiet and restful as Maine or Michigan woods," was marketed to Cleveland residents in the early twentieth century by R. Schenkel.

New Construction

17. A covered bridge stood at this site until 1897, but it is not among those documented with a number. The existing sandstone abutments were modified for the new covered bridge.

BIBLIOGRAPHY

Anonymous. "Transportation." Research paper on file with the Jefferson Historical Society as part of the Early Roads and Bridges in Ashtabula County collection. Compiled in the year 2001 by the Ashtabula County Historical Society from Ashtabula County newspapers.

Ashtabula Beacon. "Highest in 20 Years." March 26, 1913.

———. "30 Foot Longer than Any Similar Bridge." July 19, 1913.

———. "Two New Bridges Over Grand River." April 17, 1913.

———. "Water Still Over Bridge at Geneva." March 26, 1913.

Ashtabula County Board of Commissioners Journal. July 18, 1867; July 4, 1835; June 7, 1819; March 4, 1857; March 4, 1856; March 6, 1850; March 13, 1819; September 15, 1878; September 24, 1818; September 2, 1856.

Ashtabula County Engineer's Office scrapbooks containing engineers' handwritten notes regarding the bridges and documentary images of bridge repairs and dismantling.

Ashtabula County Genealogical Society. *Ashtabula County History, Then and Now: A History of the People of the County by the People of the County.* Dallas, TX: Taylor Publishing Company, 1985.

Ashtabula News. "Flood." September 19, 1878.

———. "Mr. Bird Chapin." May 2, 1878.

———. "Mr. Whitney." July 18, 1878.

Ashtabula Sentinel. "Another Accident." August 31, 1926.

———. "Ashtabula Creek." June 19, 1857.

———. "Bridge Notice." January 6, 1849.

Ashtabula Star-Beacon. "Blaze Destroys Span Across Grand River." September 29, 1938.

———. "A Bridge Is Born." June 14, 1995.

———. "Bridge Spans River in 1852–1863." October 29, 1928.

BIBLIOGRAPHY

———. "County Urges Whitman's Creek...for State Park." February 22, 1946.
———. "Covered Bridge to Be Burned." May 4, 1971.
———. "Days of Crooked Gulf Bridge Limited." September 15, 1948.
———. Editorial. May 5, 1955.
———. "Efforts Being Made to Preserve Bridges." October 12, 1969.
———. "Forman Road Span May Be Moved." March 1, 1973.
———. "Geneva Unveils Big Project: One Short Covered Bridge." October 9, 2007.
———. "His Covered Bridge Leads to Pizza Palace." August 17, 1975.
———. "Mill Creek Crossing Reborn." April 18, 2009.
———. "Modern Efficiency Dooms More of Ashtabula County's Remaining Historical Bridges." September 17, 1947.
———. "100 Watch Old Bridge Burn." May 7, 1971.
———. "Plymouth Man Recalls Construction of Caine Road Bridge." May 3, 2009.
———. "Regional Press Magazine, Graham Road Bridge Moved." August 14, 1971.
———. "Rehabilitating the Past." March 24, 2004.
———. "Rock Creek Fears Fate of 109-Year-Old Covered Bridge." April 15, 1941.
———. "Ryland Series on Covered Bridges." October 10, 1960.
———. "16 Covered Bridges Left; All Crumbling." October 11, 1969.
———. "Smolen-Gulf Dedication Souvenir Supplement." August 26, 2008.
———. "Vandalism at Bridges." November 25, 1962.
———. "Wiswell Road Covered Bridge, Built in 1867, Is Rededicated." May 16, 2004.
———. "Yesterday's Bridge." January 23, 2001.
Ashtabula Weekly Telegraph. "Accident." August 27, 1870.
———. "County Commissioners." August 5, 1871.
———. "Good Sleighing." January 15, 1870.
———. "New Bridge." December 17, 1870.
———. "Planking." September 30, 1871.
Bennett, Lola. *Covered Bridges NHL Context Study*. United States Department of the Interior, National Park Service. http://www.nps.gov/nhl/Spring2012Nominations/CoveredBridgesContext.pdf.
Biographical History of Northeastern Ohio. Chicago: Lewis Publishing Company, 1893. Available at Platt R. Spencer Memorial Archives & Special Collections, Geneva, Ohio.
Bliss, Alice. *Covered Bridges* newspaper series. Ashtabula County Covered Bridge Festival Committee files, Jefferson Historical Society Resource Room, Jefferson, Ohio.
———. *Dams and Bridges* newspaper series. Ashtabula County Covered Bridge Festival Committee files, Jefferson Historical Society Resource Room.
Caswell, Bill. Covered Spans of Yesteryear. http://lostbriges.org.
Clark, Ella Francis. *History of Mechanicsville*. Oral history from January 24, 1929, on file at Platt R. Spencer Memorial Archives & Special Collections, Geneva, Ohio.
Cleveland Press. "Bridges to Past Nestle in Ohio County." November 9, 1961.
Conneaut Reporter. "Flooding." September 19, 1878.
———. March 8, 1866.
Corts, Thomas E., ed. *Bliss and Tragedy: The Ashtabula Railway-Bridge Accident of 1876 and the Loss of P.P. Bliss*. Birmingham, AL: Sherman Oak Books, popular

Bibliography

reading from Samford University Press to benefit Jennie Munger Gregory Memorial Museum, 2003.

Dillon, Edythe. *Bits and Pieces: More Stories About Wayne Township, Ashtabula County, Ohio, and Its People*. Wayne Township, OH: Wayne Township Historical Society, 1988. Available at Jefferson Historical Society Resource Room.

———. *Wayne Township, Ohio, 175th Anniversary*. Wayne Township, OH: Wayne Township Historical Society, 1978. Available at Jefferson Historical Society Resource Room.

Ellsworth, Catherine. *Ellsworth's Historical Sketches of Ashtabula Co., Ohio*. N.p.: self-published, 1988. Available at Platt R. Spencer Memorial Archives & Special Collections, Geneva, Ohio.

Foster, Emily, ed. *The Ohio Frontier: An Anthology of Early Writings*. Lexington: University Press of Kentucky, 1996.

Fritsch, James T. *The Untried Life: The 29th Ohio Volunteer Infantry in the Civil War*. Athens: Ohio University Press, 2012.

Geneva Free Press. "Stone Quarrying Recalled as Former Windsor Industry." December 3, 1930.

Geneva Free Press Times. "Wooden Bridge at Grand River." April 22, 1913; May 17, 1913.

Hagar, Joseph C., ed. *Pioneer Sketches of Madison Township, Lake County, Ohio*. Ancestry.com. http://www.rootsweb.ancestry.com/~ohlake/history/SketchesMadison.pdf.

Hakala, Paul. Scrapbooks available at the Jefferson Historical Society Resource Room.

Hall, John, Reverend. "An Early History of Ashtabula Township." Serialized in Ashtabula County newspapers in the late 1800s, copy in author's collection.

Harpersfield Heritage Society. *Harpersfield Covered Bridge: A Commemorative History*. Harpersfield Township, OH: Harpersfield Heritage Society, 1991. Available at the Jefferson Historical Society Resource Room, Jefferson, Ohio.

Hatcher, Harlan. *The Western Reserve: The Story of New Connecticut in Ohio*. Kent, OH: Kent State University Press, 1991.

Iron and Early Steel Truss Bridges in Ohio. "Historic Bridge Survey for Ohio (2007)." Ohio Historic Bridge Association. http://oldohiobridges.com/OHBI2007.xls.

———. Ohio Historic Bridge Association. http://oldohiobridges.com.

Jefferson Gazette. "Long Way Around for Pioneer Traveller." September 6, 1960.

———. "Mill Creek Bridge at Williams Corner." February 14, 1961.

———. "New Bridge at Dorset." March 11, 1930.

Jefferson Sentinel. "Proposal Would Save Covered Bridges." March 26, 1980.

Kennedy, James Harrison. *A History of the City of Cleveland: Its Settlement, Rise and Progress, 1796–1896*. Cleveland State University Libraries. http://www.clevelandmemory.org/ebooks/kennedy.

Lake, D.J., surveyor. *Atlas of Ashtabula County, Ohio*. Philadelphia, PA: Titus, Simmons & Titus, 1874. Available at Jefferson Historical Society Resource Room.

Large, Monia W. *Volume I: History of Ashtabula County, Ohio, in Two Volumes*. Topeka, KS: Historical Publishing Company, 1924.

Bibliography

Longfellow, Rickie. "Back in Time: Ohio's Vanishing Covered Bridges." U.S. Department of Transportation, Federal Highway Administration. http://www.fhwa.dot.gov/infrastructure/back0804.cfm.

Lyon, Jean. "Fresh from the Nineteenth Century." *Western Reserve* magazine (November–December 1983).

Meredith, Pauline B., and Edwin E. Rawdon. *Ashtabula County Historical Society Quarterly Bulletin* 1, no. 4 (December 29, 1954). On file at Platt R. Spencer Memorial Archives & Special Collections, Geneva, Ohio.

Metcalf, Dave. "The Short Story of Mechanicsville and Its Bridge," 1984. On file at Platt R. Spencer Memorial Archives & Special Collections, Geneva, Ohio.

Ohio History. "March 13–27, 1913: Statewide Flood." http://ww2.ohiohistory.org/etcetera/exhibits/swio/pages/content/1913_flood.htm.

Osborn, Dennis. List of Ashtabula County timber bridges. On file at Jefferson Historical Society.

Seeley, Bill. Transcript of radio interview recorded in 1980s. On file at Platt R. Spencer Memorial Archives & Special Collections, Geneva, Ohio.

Sloane, Eric. *American Barns and Covered Bridges.* New York: Wilfred Funk Inc., 1954.

Tennessee Department of Transportation. "Covered Bridges in Tennessee—What is a Truss Bridge?" http://www.tdot.state.tn.us/bridges/trussbridges.htm.

Travis, Dale J. Search results for Ohio covered bridges. http://dalejtravis.com.

U.S. Census Records. Ashtabula County, Ohio, 1830–1920. http://www.censusrecords.com.

Wickham, Gertrude Van Rensselaer. *Memorial to the Pioneer Women of the Western Reserve.* Published monthly under the auspices of the Woman's Department of the Cleveland Centennial Commission, 1896.

Wikipedia. "Covered Bridge." http://en.wikipedia.org/wiki/Covered_bridge.

———. "Great Dayton Flood." http://en.wikipedia.org/wiki/Great_Dayton_Flood.

Williams Brothers. *History of Ashtabula County, Ohio: With Illustrations and Biographical Sketches of Its Pioneers and Most Prominent Men.* Philadelphia, PA: Williams Brothers, 1878.

Wood, Miriam. *The Covered Bridges of Ohio: An Atlas and History.* Columbus, OH: Old Trail Printing Company, 1993.

Wright, David W., ed. *World Guide to Covered Bridges.* Concord, NH: National Society for the Preservation of Covered Bridges Inc., 2009.

INDEX

A

Abbott, E.T. 75
Ackley, Samuel 30, 31, 74
Adams, Charles 47
Adams Road bridge 47–48
Alderman, Ada 71
Alderman School 71
Alderman School bridge 70–71
Amidon, Samuel 41
arson 42, 63
Ashtabula County
  early bridges of 21–23
  early roads of 21–23
  waterways of 14–16
Ashtabula County Antique Engine
    Club 111
Ashtabula County commissioners
  bridge construction 21–23
  bridge renovation 81–84
Ashtabula County Fairgrounds 128
Ashtabula County Joint Vocational
    School 121
Ashtabula County Metroparks 92
"Ashtabula Horror, The" 26
Ashtabula Main River Crossing bridge
    38–39

Ashtabula River 15
  bridges of 87, 92, 101, 103, 112,
    121, 125
  Gulf, the 34, 38, 114, 117, 120
  lost bridges of 38–50
Ashtabula-Trumbull Turnpike 74
Ashtabula, Youngstown & Pittsburgh
    Railroad 126
Atkins, Quintus 21

B

Benetka, James 84
Benetka Road bridge 84–87
  repairs to 37
Benson, Albert 90
Benson, Robert 90–92
Bentley 29, 72
Black Diamond Railroad 50
Blaine Road bridge 41–42
Blanchard, Aaron 94
Bliss, Alice 40, 46, 55, 61, 64, 69, 71,
    72, 80
Bliss, P.P. 26
Blodgett, Caleb 44
Bobwood Valley 42
BOG Construction 113

INDEX

bog iron 53
Bottorf, Barrie 99–101, 129
Bottorf, Fred 100, 129
Bottorf, Naomi Olin 129
Brick Layers and Allied Trades Local 16 120
Burke, Parsons, Bowlby 113
Burr arch 24, 95
Burr, Theodore 24

C

Caine Road bridge 109–112
Callender Road East bridge 76
Callender Road West bridge 57
Camp Peet 88
Carpenters Local 95 120
Cemetery Creek 16
Christy bridge 59
Christy, James 59
Civil War 51, 66
Clark, Ella Francis 97
Clark's Corners 53
Clark's Mill 84
Cleaveland, Moses 16, 17
Cochran, Ryan 116–121
Cold Springs bridge 64
Collins bridge 66
Comprehensive Employment Training Act 108
Conneaut Creek 15
  bridges of 87–88, 97–99, 107–109, 125
  early timber trestle across 51
  lost bridges of 50–56
Cornish-Windsor 115
Covered Bridge Festival 94, 101, 123, 128
"Covered Bridge Lady" 129
Covered Bridge Pizza Parlor 66–69
covered bridges (legacy)
  accidents at 14, 60, 66, 73
  arson 42, 63
  attempts to save 61, 75, 76
  builders of Ashtabula County ones 27–32
  burning of 76
  construction techniques 26, 91, 96, 109, 112
  cost to build 32
  customs 14
  damage by vehicles 63, 73, 80
  dating of 86
  development of 23
  maintenance of 37, 92
  museums 129
  nighttime photography of 9
  on private property 127
  reasons for covering 13
  souvenirs 129
  state responsibility for 69, 93
  swimming holes 99
  truss types 24–27, 110, 113
  vandalism 106
  wind loading 52, 102
  wood types 26, 111
Cowles, Beverly 114
Cowles Creek 121
Cox, George 60
Cox Road 71
cranes, use of building bridges 109, 111, 113, 119
Creek Road bridge 87–88
Crooked Gulf bridge 40–41, 114, 120
Crowell, George 30, 31, 74
Crowell, William 31

D

DeVivo, Dr. Angelo 121
Dewey Road bridge. *See* Olin bridge
Dillon, Edythe 72
Dodgeville Road bridge 128
Dorset bridge 65–66
  accidents at 14, 65–66
Doyle Road bridge 88–89

E

Eagleville bridge (Forman Road) 66–69
East Trumbull bridge 77–78

INDEX

Eldridge, David 96
Ellsworth, Robert "Bob" 42, 109–112

F

Fairfield County, Ohio 12
Farnham, Elisha 51
Farnham twin bridges 50–52
Federal Intermodal Surface Transportation Efficiency Act 113
Ferrying rates 19
Fleming, Terry 60
float bridges 22
floods 32–35
  1818 32
  1837 32
  1857 33
  1878 34, 51, 78, 126
  1913 34, 57, 90, 93, 95
Foot, Roger 57
Forman Road. *See* Eagleville bridge
Fortney Road 63
Friedstrom, Edwin and Debbie 117
Frog Alley 63
Fuller's Mill 51
Furnace Road bridge 53–54

G

Gageville bridge 42–43
Gallagher bridge 128
Giddings Road bridge 112–113
Giddings Run 16
Girdled Road
  construction of 18
Gould covered bridge 29, 48–50
Graf, Robert 97
Graham Road bridge 90–92
Grandbouche, Julie 129
Grand River 14
  boat operation on 59
  bridges of 92–97, 101–102
  lost bridges of 57–64
  "great crossing, the" 96
Grigg's Creek 69

H

Hakala, Paul 50
Harper, Alexander 17
Harpersfield bridge 92–94
  damage to 37
  stone for 28
Hart family 72
Hatcher, Harlan 16
Haupt truss 113
Hayward, Samuel 28, 29, 44
Hewitt, B.F. 93
Hewitt, Gary 66–69
Hiestan, Christine 128
Hildom Road bridge 45–46
Horton, Dean 97
Howe Bridge and Truss Company 27
Howe truss 27, 97
Humphrey, Ambrose 57, 97

I

Indian Trails Park 38, 40, 114

J

Jack, Walter 38, 47
Johnson Road 59
Johnston, Mike 122

K

Kelloggsville bridge 45
Ketchum Road bridge 128
kingpost 23, 121
Koski Construction 117
Kreig 30

L

Labor Local 245 120
Lago, Bill 122
Lake Shore & Michigan Southern Railroad 26–27, 125–126
laminated wood girders, reinforcing bridge with 102, 103
Laskey Road bridge 128
Lepper, Mr. 60

Index

Long, Stephen H. 26
Lukas, Carl 89
Lynch, Jordan 122

M

Mahoning Coal Railroad 125
March Road bridge 69–70
Martin, Tim 115
Massillon Bridge and Structural Company 59
Matson's mill 54
McMurphy, Brandon 122
McMurphy, Jack 122
Meade, Abel 50
Mechanicsville bridge 95–97
Mechanicsville fire 97
Merry Isle 59
Metcalf, John 19
Middle Road bridge 97–99
Mill Creek 15
   bridges of 88–89, 104, 112–114, 126
Miller, Harry 75
Mills Creek 15
Mill Street bridge 52
Mollick, Mark 109
"Mr. Covered Bridge" 81
Mullen bridge 89
Munger, Herb 91

N

National Register of Historic Places 94
National Society for the Preservation of Covered Bridges 38
Netcher Road bridge 113–114
New Hudson Road bridge 64
"Night Crossings" 130
Northern Ohio Covered Bridge Society 42, 61

O

Ohio Historic Bridge Association 11
Ohio Public Works Commission 116, 121
Old Girdled Road 96
Old Plank bridge 62–63
Old Plank Road 62
Old Salt Road 18
Olin, Almon 99
Olin bridge 99–101, 129
Olin Museum of Covered Bridges 129
Operators Local 18 120
Ormsby, Johnson 49
Ormsby, Volney H. 29, 49
Oxley, David and Jeanne 126

P

Pearson, Jim 121
Peck, Marion 84
pedestrian walkways 94, 114
Pennsylvania Railroad 125–126
Phelps Creek
   bridges of 105–106
Pierpont bridge 46–47
"Pike, the" 42
Plank Road Company 23
Platform bridge 85
Potter family 29–30, 88, 100
Potter, Lemuel 30
Pratt truss 110, 115
Prim's Sawmill 69–70
Pymatuning Creek 16, 71–73
   lost bridge of 71–73
Pymatuning Lake 128

Q

queen post 24

R

railroad bridges, timber 125–126
Ransom, Caroline 94
Ransom, John 94
Ransomville 94
Rathbone and Skinner 52
Reynard, Bill 11
Righter Construction 113
Riverdale Road bridge 101–102
   damage to 37
"Road of Remembrance" 42

INDEX

Roaming Rock Lake 76
Rock Creek 16
  lost bridges of 73–77
Rock Creek bridge 30, 73–75
Rogers, James H. 31, 85
Roman arch bridge 64
Rome Township 63
Rome two-lane bridge 63–64
Root Road bridge 102–103
Route 6 double bridge 63–64
Route 322 Orwell East bridge 76–77
Route 322 Orwell West bridge 59–60

S

saw marks and bridge dating 86
Schmidt, Phil and Cathie 121
Schwartz, Ruben 121
Sentinel Structures 113, 118, 122
Seymour and Giddings 32
Shaffer bridge 57–59
Shaffer, John 58
Shafferville 58
Shenango Creek 128
Sherman's Mill 54
Sloane, Eric 23
Smolen, Andrew 118
Smolen-Gulf bridge 114–121
Smolen, John, Jr. 80–81
  new bridge construction 114–123
  plan to save bridges 83–84
  renovation plan 97
South Denmark Road bridge 104
South Ridge 19
South Ridge bridge 54–55
South Windsor Road 62
Spring Street bridge 39
stagecoaches 19
Stanhope-Kelloggsville Road 44, 103
Stanton, Howard 86
State Road bridge 107–109
Steamburg 49
Stewart, Robert 27, 51
Stone, Amasa 27
stone quarries 28
Stoney Creek 125

stringer bridges 127
Sullivan, Patrick 28
Sutliff, Doreen 128

T

Tannery Hill Road 38
Thompson, Mrs. J.P. 73
Tomlinson, Joseph 27
Tote Road bridge 127
Town, Ithiel 24
Town truss 26
Trumbull bridge 79
Trumbull Creek
  lost bridges of 77–79
Turney, Asa S. 17

U

Underwood Road 71
Union Industrial Contractors 95, 121
Urch, Duane 96

V

Vaux, Tammy 118
Vorse, Guy 97

W

walking bridge 93
Warner Hollow 105–106. *See* Wiswell
    bridge
Waters, Norma 15
Watson, Brad and Holly 129
Way, Vinton 64
Western Reserve, Connecticut 17
Western Reserve Greenway Trail 126
Westfall, Stanley 113
West Liberty bridge 121–123
Whitman Creek 79
Whitman Creek bridge 79–80
Wick bridge 71–73
Wild and Scenic Rivers 15
Williams bridge 69
Williams Corners 104
Windsor Road 64
Windsor Road bridge 64

Wing, Paul and Jeanne 84
Wing, Tim 87
Winship, T.S. 28, 29, 32, 44, 48
Wiswell Road (Warner Hollow) bridge
    105–106
Woods Road 18

Y

Young's mill 32

ABOUT THE AUTHOR

Carl E. Feather is a veteran print journalist and photographer who worked for the *Ashtabula Star Beacon* and *Conneaut (OH) News-Herald* for nearly thirty years. He is a frequent contributor to *Goldenseal* magazine, published by the West Virginia Department of Culture and History. Carl has produced numerous video documentary programs on northeast Ohio and West Virginia topics, and he blogs about regional history at thefeathercottage.com.

Carl and his wife, Amanda, live in Ashtabula, and he works in tourism development for the Ashtabula County Board of Commissioners.

Visit us at
www.historypress.net

This title is also available as an e-book

www.ingramcontent.com/pod-product-compliance
Lightning Source LLC
Chambersburg PA
CBHW042143160426
43201CB00022B/2387